"Ed deftly weaves together a lifetime's experiences and observations: a memoir of a pioneering ultramarathoner and professional writer, a primer of advice on going long distances, an anthropological study of humans as runners, and a set of environmental/ecological essays. Each topic alone would have made a good book. Together they yield a great one, richly detailed and finely written."

—JOE HENDERSON, former editor, *Runner's World*

■ ■ ■

"An epic story of how important our fitness as individuals may be to the long-run sustainability of our national and global society."

—JACQUELINE HANSEN, two-time world-record holder
for the women's marathon, Boston Marathon winner,
and first woman to run a sub-2:40 marathon

■ ■ ■

"Ayres's tale is nothing less than a philosophical treatise on how to survive and thrive in a world of dwindling resources, alarming climate change, and haunting violence. It's about a human race, but also *the* human race."

—LARRY SHAPIRO, PhD, author of *Zen and the Art of Running*

■ ■ ■

"This is a story of critical connections—about the dawning realization that we need to rediscover how to think not just *on* our feet but *with* our feet."

—THOM HARTMANN, host of the Thom Hartmann radio and TV shows

■ ■ ■

"In a culture addicted to quick hits, fast times, and unrelenting over-stimulus, Ed Ayres speaks with the voice of wisdom, simplicity, and acceptance of what is. We highly recommend this book to anyone ready to step off the speeding train and do a freefall into the present."

—DANNY and KATHERINE DREYER, authors of
Chi Running, Chi Walking, and *Chi Marathon*

■ ■ ■

ALSO BY ED AYRES

God's Last Offer: Negotiating for a Sustainable Future

Crossing the Energy Divide: Moving from Fossil Fuel Dependence to a Clean-Energy Future
(with Robert U. Ayres)

The Worldwatch Reader on Global Environmental Issues
(Co-editor, with Lester R. Brown)

And Then the Vulture Eats You: True Tales About Ultramarathons and Those Who Run Them
(Contributor)

Imagine What America Could Be in the 21st Century: Visions of a Better Future from Leading American Thinkers
(Contributor)

ED AYRES

THE LONGEST RACE

A Lifelong Runner,

an Iconic Ultramarathon,

and the Case for

Human Endurance

THE EXPERIMENT
NEW YORK

The Experiment, LLC
260 Fifth Avenue
New York, NY 10001–6408
www.theexperimentpublishing.com

The Experiment's books are available at special discounts when purchased in bulk for premiums and sales promotions as well as for fundraising or educational use. For details, contact us at info@theexperimentpublishing.com.

Many of the designations used by manufacturers and sellers to distinguish their products are claimed as trademarks. Where those designations appear in this book and The Experiment was aware of a trademark claim, the designations have been capitalized.

Library of Congress Cataloging-in-Publication Data

Ayres, Ed.
The longest race : a lifelong runner, an iconic ultramarathon, and the case for human endurance / Ed Ayres.
       p. cm.
Includes bibliographical references.
ISBN 978-1-61519-063-8 (pbk.) – ISBN 978-1-61519-161-1 (ebook)
1. Marathon running. I. Title.
GV1065.A97 2012
796.42'52–dc23

                                                                    2012017075

ISBN 978-1-61519-063-8
Ebook ISBN 978-1-61519-161-1

Jacket design by Jen O'Connor
Jacket photograph © Jack Gescheidt | JackPhoto.com
Author photograph © Michael Asmar | Joie de Vivre Photography
Text design by Pauline Neuwirth, Neuwirth & Associates, Inc.

Manufactured in the United States of America
Distributed by Workman Publishing Company, Inc.
Distributed simultaneously in Canada by Thomas Allen and Son Ltd.
First published October 2012
10 9 8 7 6 5 4 3 2 1

CONTENTS

to Frederick

South
Mountain
Trailhead

Boonsboro
START

5 mi.

Keedysvill

N E S W

● St. James

Taylor's
Landing

to
Hagerstown

50 miles

45 miles

40 mi.

FINISH
Williamsport

Dam
4

BATTLE OF
FALLING WATER

The
JFK 50-MILE
Ultramarathon Course

THE
LONGEST
RACE

1

BOONSBORO, DAWN

The Start—When Life Begins Again

I DON'T REMEMBER being born. I doubt that anyone does. But I wonder if the moment you push off from the starting line of a long-distance footrace might be a subliminal replay of that long-forgotten launch of a new life. As the big moment approaches, you're jammed up behind an unyielding human wall—the too-close backs of other runners' necks, shoulder blades, elbows, thighs, and calves not *quite* ready to let you surge forward. You're about as naked as climate and social convention will allow, and at the same time you may feel your shoulders and hips bumping unavoidably against other shoulders and hips that are not yours but that, in a way, you feel kinship with. Then suddenly you're breaking free, and the long journey—in the company of others, but very much on your own—has begun.

There's magic in a moment like this. It's not only like being reborn each time you race; it's like having been given the secret to the most astonishing means of propulsion ever to appear on earth. And, arguably, that's what the human body offers, as many endurance runners are discovering. A horse can't compare. A bald eagle can't compare. For that matter, even a 24,500-mile-per-hour Apollo rocket to the moon couldn't have compared. Now, as I waited at the starting line, it struck me that our long-lost president John F. Kennedy, whose vision had brought that Apollo rocket into being, might be pleased by what we were about to attempt here in this fifty-mile trail race that had borne his name for the nearly four decades since his assassination.

It was late November 2001. The World Trade Center had been destroyed just over two months earlier, and the country had been staggered by the shock. But life goes on. There were a lot of Marines in this race, and no well-trained runner needed to be reminded that "when the going gets tough, the tough get going"—a credo generally attributed to President Kennedy's father, Joseph P. Kennedy. Elite Marine distance runners were as tough a breed as you'd find on this planet, and as we waited for the countdown I could see that the guys in red and gold were poised to take off like cannon shots. God help any baby who's born quite like that.

Along with the seven-man All Marines and Quantico Marines teams, there were contingents from the US Naval Academy and the army's 82nd Airborne Division, among others. The military presence at this race had been strong since the first running in 1963, maybe because it was JFK's challenge to the Marines in 1962—*see if you can walk fifty miles in a day, like Teddy Roosevelt's Marines did*—that had been the original inspiration. At the time, Kennedy had reason to fear that the physical fitness of the American military was in severe decline. But this year, in the wake of 9/11, the "when the going gets tough" spirit seemed almost palpable.

A few yards away, I spotted Frank Probst, a guy I'd had a competitive rivalry with for most of the past decade. Frank was fifty-seven and still worked at army headquarters—although what he did there I didn't know. On that blue-sky September morning nine weeks ago, he had just stepped through an exit on the southwest side of the Pentagon, on his way to another part of the building, when a Boeing 757 roared very low across the adjacent road, coming *straight at him.* As it clipped off a utility pole, he threw himself to the ground and the plane missed him by about fifteen feet before exploding through the Pentagon's massive concrete wall. In the following days, as the attack's prime surviving witness, he'd had to replay his near-death experience in intensive interrogation, but now here he was—ready to run.

My reasons for entering this race were as complex—or simple—as my reasons for wanting to be alive. I'd been a competitive long-distance runner for the past forty-four years, and I was undeniably addicted. I had also just turned sixty, and it can feel disconcerting to a man at that age to find that he no longer has the strength or mojo that he once had, and that has always seemed an essential part of who he is. Part of my motivation was that I wanted to see if I could still run with guys who were in their twenties or thirties—or even forties. I had reasons to think maybe I could.

Possibly the biggest reason I was standing here, though, was about that most irreducible of all human needs—the instinct to survive. An ultramarathon race, or *ultra,* (any footrace longer than a marathon) is a ritual of survival. In a world beset by ever-more ominous threats—now heightened by those tragic events of two months ago—the need to not just hope and plan intelligently but to actively practice the art of survival had put a tightening grip on me.

Nearly a thousand marathon-hardened runners were

entered—the maximum number the government would allow to run on the Appalachian Trail. I was one of the oldest people in the field, but I knew I had two advantages. First, I might well be the most *experienced* runner in this race, if not in the whole country, and I wanted to find out to what extent experience could trump youth, or at least keep pace with it. Our culture was more and more dominated by youth, and I frankly needed to know if I still counted. In a short-distance run, or sprint, there was little—well, nothing—an old guy could do to compete with a twenty- or twenty-five-year-old. Guys my age, no matter how tough or strong they might be, could never play wide receiver for the Redskins or Steelers, catching passes and sprinting for touchdowns. In a *long* run, though, it might be a different story. Maybe my experience could give me an edge.

The second advantage I had stemmed from the work I'd done for the past ten years at the Worldwatch Institute in Washington, DC, as an editor, parsing research reports from environmental scientists documenting what appeared to be the declining stability and sustainability of our civilization. Over the years, I'd noticed curious parallels between the ecology of human societies under duress and that of an individual human under great stress. I had begun to wonder, *are these parallels more than just coincidence?* Earlier in my career, I'd spent seven years editing research reports for several of the pioneers of the environmental movement and had my first inklings that survival wasn't just an abstract, academic concept of interest to biology students studying Darwin; it was very here and now. Although most of the general public seemed oblivious, the scientists I worked with (and many others I would correspond with in later years) were deeply alarmed. The first scientist I'd done editing for, in the 1970s, was the nuclear physicist Theodore B. (Ted) Taylor, who earlier in his career, at Los Alamos, had designed the largest fission atomic bomb ever exploded on earth—the so-called Super Oralloy bomb, which was detonated over Enewetak Atoll in the Pacific in 1953 with a power thirty-seven times that of the bomb we dropped on Hiroshima. Dr. Taylor had also designed the *smallest* atomic bomb ever exploded—the so-called suitcase bomb, which could fit in the trunk of a car. By the time I met him, he had renounced that legacy and was laboring to warn the world of the dangers of nuclear leaks, thefts, accidents, and terrorism. He had surmised, several years ago, that the World Trade Center might be a prime target for terrorists armed with a suitcase bomb like the one *he* had designed.

Taylor's journal, which I was hired to edit, was distributed to all the national and international nuclear agencies—none of which seemed much interested in his warnings. There was a lot of money to be made in the new industry of nuclear power, and there were well-lubricated revolving doors between the nuclear agencies and utilities. The editing work was both intense and frustrating, and after work each evening I'd go out for long runs along the DC bank of the Potomac. Running gave me a needed escape, but at the same time I found myself meditating on those remarkable parallels I saw between our fast-growing global industries and our overstressed selves.

Now, a quarter of a century later, I was in a position to draw on what I'd learned about the nature of human capability, whether to power missiles or propel our own bodies, and to use that knowledge to run faster than I once would have thought possible for a man my age. Did that mean what I could do as a runner was now more important to me than what I could do for my embattled planet? Not really. But I had no control over what happened at the Nuclear Regulatory

Commission, or International Atomic Energy Agency, or US Department of Energy—where, for all I knew, Ted Taylor's reports were just being fed to the shredder. I could at least have some control over what I did with my own body and soul. And in the long run, I thought, that might be what really counts.

■ ■ ■

We were tightly crowded together, the top-seeded guys in the front row using whatever subtle hip-bumping or leaning was needed to hold their places behind the white line, while the rest of us jammed as close as possible behind them on the narrow street. We were a sea of bare arms and legs and, despite the cold, even a few bare shoulders of road-racer types wearing singlets instead of high-tech T-shirts. There were men and women of all ages here, but the great majority were twenty to forty years younger than I. The sight of the younger ones bouncing up and down on their forefeet to keep warm threw my memory back to when I was their age. I felt too old now to be bouncing; I might need that bounce in the last mile.

I had started running with high school cross-country and track in the 1950s, followed by college cross-country and my first road races in the 1960s, when new chapters of the Road Runners Club of America were springing up all over the country, and eventually I'd gotten hooked on marathons. The first time I'd ever heard of an *ultra*marathon was in the early 1970s, when there were only a handful of ultras in the whole country. Now, at the outset of the twenty-first century, there were about five hundred ultras each year in the US— mostly on rugged rural or wilderness trails, far from public view. The JFK 50 Mile was—and is—the country's oldest and largest.

The JFK 50 began in the spring of 1963 as an unpublicized personal venture for a group of eleven men who initially called it the "JFK 50 Mile Challenge"—one of many so-named events that took place that year and the winter before in response to President Kennedy's challenge to the Marines. After the assassination in 1963, all the others discontinued, but this one quietly expanded—perhaps in part because of where it took place. The course the original group chose was both rich in natural wonders and redolent of American military history. It started right here where we were standing, in Boonsboro, Maryland, a town that had been founded by two cousins of the pioneer Daniel Boone a few years after the Revolutionary War. It followed the historic National Road up a long hill to a forested ridge where the civil war Battle of South Mountain left 5,867 men dead, wounded, or missing in action over at least six miles of the mountain's spine in 1862; eventually dropped down a precipitous escarpment to the Potomac River near Harpers Ferry, where John Brown attacked the US Arsenal in 1859 and was defeated by the Marines under the command of General Robert E. Lee; wended north along the C&O Canal Towpath past Antietam Battlefield, the site of the bloodiest day in American military history with a total of 23,000 casualties and with Lee now commanding the other side; passed Pack Horse Ford, where the surviving Confederates escaped across the Potomac after the bloodbaths at Antietam and Sharpsburg; left the Potomac River at one of the five dams the opposing armies struggled to control; and followed a rolling country road to the town of Williamsport, which George Washington visited in 1790 when it was being considered as a possible capital city for the United States.

The JFK 50 quickly became an iconic event among endurance runners, even as it remained virtually unknown to the sports media or public. By the 1990s, when ultras usually had at most a few hundred entrants, the JFK had to limit its field to a thousand. For the original race director, Buzz Sawyer, and his successor, Mike Spinnler, the JFK was a logistical challenge that the Civil War generals McClellan, Lee, and Stonewall Jackson, among others who knew this terrain, might have quite respected—helping a thousand men and women who were determined to run fifty miles in less than a day to achieve their goals without anyone dropping dead. By 2001, Spinnler had established a well-orchestrated routine: As his army of volunteers dispersed to their assigned positions at aid stations, medical tents, radio communications, and course monitoring posts, the runners and support crews would arrive at the Boonsboro High School in the predawn chill, gather in the gym to keep warm, then at 6:40 AM—still a little dark—take off their warm-ups, leave the gym, and walk three-fourths of a mile to the middle of the town, where a white line was painted across the street. The start would be at 7:00 sharp—right at sunrise. For many, the goal would be to reach Williamsport before dark returned, which in late November would be around 4:30 PM—a finishing time of 9 hours, 30 minutes. About half of the runners wouldn't make it until later, well after dark. You had 14 hours to finish before being disqualified. The fastest any man over sixty (my age bracket) had run this race, in its thirty-eight years so far, was 8 hours and 14 minutes. My goal—which I hoped wasn't just pie in the sky—was to finish under 8 hours.

So here we were, about to go forth like that newborn infant feeling the first rush of air into its lungs, beginning its own magical journey. Life is a mystery from the get-go, no less so for a runner at the start of a long race. Though I'd been experiencing this kind of moment for more years than anyone else here, I still marveled at the mental challenges—if nothing else, the challenges to just plain sanity and common sense. In the warm gym, we had huddled in our sweats and hoodies, yet now we stood in face-freezing cold wearing almost nothing. We were here to compete, yet there was no smack talk of the sort that seemed so common now in sports; with just a couple of minutes to go, runners were shaking hands, wishing each other well. And for all of us, this would be a deadly serious undertaking, yet there was an undercurrent of joshing and joking: "Excuse me, is this the line for coffee?"

Once, in the 1980s, I had met Muhammad Ali at the start of the Los Angeles Marathon, and he seemed to grasp, in a way that took me quite by surprise, the good-humored camarade- rie of runners about to compete. I was there to report on the event for *Running Times* (a magazine I had founded in 1977 and still did some writing for), and when I climbed onto the photographers' platform overlooking the starting area, who should I see but the world's most legendary athlete, who'd been brought in to fire the starting gun. I shook his hand and asked, awkwardly, "So, what do you think of all these thousands of people warming up to run twenty-six miles?" I expected him to say something appropriate to the ceremonial nature of his presence, such as "It's a great thing; it's inspiring!" Instead, Ali fixed me with that baleful stare he'd so often laid on reporters, and said, "They got to be crazy!" I laughed, a bit nervously. I knew it was just a little jab, but it was a *Muhammad Ali* jab, and I was still on my feet! Remembering that now at the start of the JFK, it occurred to me—in the spirit of the moment—that if marathoners are crazy, people who run fifty miles on trails must be *twice* as crazy.

The guy with the bullhorn announced that we had thirty seconds, and then at 6:59:50 he began a countdown: "Ten, nine, eight . . ." It was time to let my mind go blank, Zenlike. This was important. Over the few days before the event, I'd done a lot of mental rehearsing and spent an inordinate amount of time thinking about the first three miles, which quickly confront you with a strategic conundrum. The first mile, like a scene from an old Western, is just *get out of town.* No problem with that. But the next two miles are a fairly steep climb to the South Mountain pass, where you leave the road and enter a thirteen-mile segment of the 2,168-mile-long Appalachian Trail (AT). The conundrum is that on one hand you want to get to the trailhead before the horde does, because the AT is a rocky, single-track path—wide enough in most places for just one runner at a time, or two at most—and if you reach this bottleneck in the same minute as several hundred other determined people, you'll be slowed like bumper-to-bumper traffic squeezing past an accident, and you'll lose a lot of time. Best to get to the trailhead ahead of the traffic, if you can do so without too much strain. On the other hand, going up the South Mountain road, it would be a big mistake to go too fast. It's a tricky thing to balance, but once the race started I wanted to be on autopilot, not burning energy trying to calculate.

"Seven, six, five . . ."

I went blank, finally, the way I had late last night at the hotel in Hagerstown, when I'd finally lapsed into a few hours of restless sleep.

2

SOUTH MOUNTAIN

The Rush—and the Dilemma of Pacing

WE RAN THROUGH the town as if in a dream. Most of the houses on this main street—once curiously known as America's National Road—were narrow wood structures that had been built over a century ago and looked abandoned now. A few even older stone houses appeared to date from the eighteenth century. A lone coffee shop had lights on, as did the temperature sign on the bank, but all the houses were dark. State police had cleared the road of cars. In minutes, we were out of town and starting up the mountain, and despite my effort to go blank I found myself thinking, *not too fast, not too fast!* I marveled at how I had once run this race, over a quarter century ago, when I was evidently too young to understand "too fast"—and somehow got away with it. At the age of thirty-six, I had run the JFK and experienced the thrill of my life by actually winning the race outright in a time of 6 hours, 4 minutes—about twelve minutes ahead of the second-place guy. That year, there'd been 483 starters, and I'd been one of the first five or six to reach the South Mountain trailhead. I still have a photo of that lead group of guys with our jaunty '70s mustaches and long hair nearing the top of the South Mountain hill, and in the photo I'm actually *smiling*. Unbelievable.

In those years the trail segment of the course was a little different than now—same distance, but a bit rougher. During the Cold War, a silo-like structure had been erected high on the ridge we would be following once we hit the trail, on "government" land accessed by a narrow, paved service road. The area around it had been closed off. The Appalachian Trail had been forced to detour around the west slope of the mountain, then climb steeply back to the ridge on the far side of the closed-off area. On the climb back up, a stretch of about twenty yards went up a rocky stream bed where the slope was almost as steep as one of those climbing walls we were now starting to see in upscale gyms, and I distinctly recalled trying to *run* up that incline in 1977—and going alarmingly anaerobic. Going anaerobic, as almost every runner knows, is what happens when you come to the end of a hard sprint. It's also called having "the bear on your back." For a short distance you fly, and then suddenly you can't. Your legs need more oxygen at that speed (or at that steepness of incline) than your lungs can take in or your blood can deliver fast enough. You're thrown into oxygen debt, and your muscles feel like they've been filled with acid—which to some degree they have, as the lactic acid by-product of fight-or-flight metabolism suddenly piles up like panicked bodies at the clogged exit of a theater on fire. Within seconds, the whole physiological system either seizes up or slows to a crawl. If you're running a long distance, going anaerobic somewhere along the way can take a heavy toll: You may have to stop, put your hands on your knees, and gulp air until the lactic acid dissipates and the oxygen debt is paid off. Somehow, on that long-ago November day, thanks to the three-a-week monster speed workouts I'd been doing, I only had to slow or walk for a few seconds before recovering.

Now, twenty-four years later, at an age when no man or woman can do three-a-week speed workouts without getting sick or breaking down, I was definitely not smiling, and there was little danger I'd let myself go anywhere *near* anaerobic. Up ahead, the trail had been restored to its pre–Cold War route, and today we would actually run on that paved service road that some locals noted was somehow always snow free in the winter. The structure was supposedly still there, and the locals called it "the missile silo"—referring to the system of about 265 missile bases that had been deployed around the US in the 1960s to protect the country from Soviet nuclear attack. When I first heard about the one up on South Mountain, I thought, in a sort of swords-to-ploughshares spirit, *How appropriate—a transformation of the ridge's use from Nike missiles to Nike running shoes!* But then I looked up a list of all the known US Nike missile silo sites, and none was listed for this part of Maryland. Apparently, the real purpose of this structure—the reason it had been fenced off all those years—was never made public.

When we reached the South Mountain pass, we would run a short distance on the Appalachian Trail before entering the unexplained service road, which evidently accessed the ridge from another part of the valley. We'd run the road's two-mile length before returning to the trail. I made a mental note to scan the woods when I reached the service road's terminus and see if there really was a silo there. Right now, though, I needed to deal with the challenge of South Mountain. Was I being too conservative? Halfway up the mountain, five or six

Marines went past me in a pack—guys young enough to do three-a-week speed workouts or, hell, *five* in a week—*ooh-rah!*—running as if they were on their way to plant a flag. *Let them go,* I thought. Some of those guys are going to come back to me soon enough.

That bit of lore—that "they'll come back to you"—had been a part of the standard distance runner's indoctrination at least since my high school cross-country days. Going out too fast at the start of a race was the classic rookie mistake. It was also something that, at big races where TV cameras or spectators were present, always seemed to bring out at least one entrant who got way too excited. At the Boston Marathon, at least in the 1960s and '70s, you'd see some guy no one had heard of take off from the start at a hell-bent sprint, clearly visible in a photo of the front-runners in the next day's *Boston Globe.* He'd have a nice clipping to show the grandchildren, although if they asked the guy "Did you win?" (that disconcerting question all runners seem to get asked), he might have had to admit that within seconds after the photo was taken, less than half a mile from the start, he had staggered off the road gasping, the bear on his back, and done for the day.

More common, though, were the runners who really did want to go the whole distance but had a poor sense of pace. And here was one of those ways that our speed-enamored culture had most conspicuously disconnected us from our nature. The poor pacers were those who'd maybe seen too many spectacular touchdown runs or cop chases on TV, and without thinking would go too fast for the first two miles of a 10K, then begin helplessly slowing down and drifting back through the field as more even-paced runners caught up. If you were one of the guys running patiently far behind, the guy who was slowing would appear to be "coming back" to you. I felt confident some of those Marines would be coming back, at least eventually.

There's always a risk that that kind of confidence can turn out to be hubris, and part of what makes endurance running an adventure is that you never know what will actually happen. But I knew that if you pay close attention to what your internal signals are telling you, they heighten your chances of actually doing what you *dream* of doing. The most fundamental education of a long-distance runner had been encapsulated over two decades ago by the iconic runner-philosopher George Sheehan, whose signature counsel was: "Listen to your body." Sheehan was a prominent cardiologist, one of the regulars at the New York Road Runners races I ran in the 1960s and '70s, and in those days it was so unusual for a medical doctor to enjoy and advocate running that we road runners listened with our jaws hanging to what Doc had to say. Instinctively, most of us knew that what we were doing was good for our hearts and health (many doctors in those days argued that it was not), and Sheehan's "Listen to your body" became a kind of mantra.

Sheehan was light-years ahead of his time. A *doctor* who ran *marathons?* When I was growing up, people thought of doctors as sedate, middle-aged white men with neatly parted graying hair who spoke and moved with measured deliberation. If they'd ever done anything athletic or acrobatic or impulsive—well, that must have been back in their youth, before med school and their professional life began. George Sheehan was white and middle-aged, but he definitely broke the mold: He ran hard, and in photos of him finishing a race in his middle years, his face is contorted like that of a man in either pain or ecstasy. The same year I won the JFK, Sheehan ran the fastest 15K in the US by anyone over the age of fifty. He ran hard and taught thousands of us how we could, too, if we'd pay attention to the biofeedback. He didn't think for a minute that a doctor knows better than your own genes how to run the astonishingly complex system that is your body. And only you can listen to the song of yourself while you're running. Pacing, so you don't burn out prematurely, is the most basic skill a distance runner learns, and pacing is all about listening to the signals that tell you whether the rates at which you are burning energy, rehydrating, getting oxygen and nutrients to the muscles, and getting rid of metabolic waste can be sustained over the distance you've chosen to race.

The Marines were almost out of sight around a bend on the hill, and once again—as I'd done hundreds of times in other races—I reminded myself of Sheehan's mantra. "Listen to your body" had become one of those casual adages that everyone respects but few runners spend much time really probing. For me it was not so easy to gloss over, in part because of a personal encounter I'd had with Sheehan half a lifetime ago, and in part because of what I'd learned in my work with environmental scientists. One spring at the Boston Marathon, I think in 1965 or '66, I went to the starting line itching to race. I'd had a great year of training—big interval workouts, fast times at weekly mid-distance (five- to ten-mile) road races—and I was primed for a marathon personal record (PR). In those days, Boston had a gauntlet of medical doctors screening the entrants (maybe on the lookout for camera-hounds who might also be latent heart-attack prospects), and you couldn't walk up to the starting line without getting a doctor's official OK. I knew I was more than OK. But then a doctor put his stethoscope to my chest and kept it there a little too long, frowning. "I can't let you run," he said finally. "You have a murmur." Devastated, I looked around for help—and who should I see warming up nearby but *George*

Sheehan. I ran to him in a panic. "Doc," I said, "They won't let me run! The guy said I have a heart murmur!"

Sheehan walked me back to the foolish doctor. This happened over a decade before Sheehan's book *Running and Being: The Total Experience* reached the *New York Times* bestseller list for a fourteen-week stay, making him a kind of sports celebrity. Even by the mid-1960s, among other doctors in the nascent field of sports medicine, Sheehan was regarded with a certain awe. The doctor looked up as we approached, and Sheehan nodded toward me and told the man, "I know this guy. He's OK to run. I'll take responsibility for him." The doctor raised his eyebrows, shrugged, and let me in. I didn't get a PR that day, but my heart ran like a Mercedes—or at least like my durable old VW. Later, Dr. Sheehan invited me to come to his Red Bank, New Jersey, office for a full cardio exam. He told me that yes, my heart did make an unusual sound, but it wasn't the kind of murmur that signals any danger. It resulted from an enlargement of the heart muscle that he'd found to be common in people who'd run many thousands of miles. He called it "athlete's heart" and assured me I had nothing to worry about.

Years later I would learn, with great amusement, that in 1911 the legendary Clarence DeMar had an encounter very similar to mine at the start of the Boston Marathon. In his 1937 memoir, *Marathon*, he recalled: "Before the race, as usual, the staff of doctors examined all the contestants and advised one or two not to start. They listened quite a while at my chest and gave the verdict that this should be my last race and I should drop out if I got tired. They said that I had heart murmurs. I do not know whether it is possible to run a marathon in competition and not get tired, but at any rate I've never done it."[1] DeMar *won* the race and later won Boston six more times. When he died in old age, doctors performed an autopsy and found that his coronary arteries were more than twice the diameter of "normal" arteries and completely free of plaque.

What impressed me most about my starting-line encounter with Dr. Sheehan was that he had been willing to vouch for me even though he'd not yet examined me himself. I had, to his evident satisfaction, *already examined myself.* In effect, he was confident—based on what he knew about me as a fellow runner, not as a patient—that I was proficient at listening to my body not just casually but in the more probing way that's essential if you want to be really good. In 1970, I ran in the inaugural New York Marathon and happily vindicated Sheehan's judgment by finishing in third place without so much as a moment of inappropriate chest pain or palpitation.

Years later, I found that what I had learned in my work with environmental scientists was providing a very different— yet strikingly parallel—confirmation that the kinds of signals Sheehan's "listen" mantra alluded to were keys to a far higher and more sustainable level of human performance than could otherwise be possible. At the same time, though, I was baffled by the apparently widening disparity between fit and unfit Americans—the growing number who were running 10Ks, riding bikes, or joining gyms, and the equally growing number who were getting "soft" in the ways JFK had publicly worried about in 1960. In an article for *Sports Illustrated,* "The Soft American," Kennedy noted that almost half of all young Americans drafted for military service were being rejected as "mentally, morally, or physically unfit."[2] He cited, among other indications, a study of muscular and flexibility tests that had been given to thousands of American and European children over a fifteen-year period, during which 57.9 percent of the American kids had failed one or more of the tests, while only 8.7 percent of the European kids had.

By the 1970s, though, the trends Kennedy worried about were affecting not just Americans, but people in other developed countries. I began to suspect that in the whole industrialized world, as our species' technological powers continued to expand and take over tasks we'd once done with our hands and legs, our capabilities as individuals were systemically weakening. Europeans and Japanese, like us, were more inclined to drive than walk, and to buy their food rather than pick it. A lot of people no longer felt any compelling *need* to be enduring.

I think I always knew subconsciously, long before I'd ever heard of ultras, that I would someday do something like this JFK run. In the years after World War II, the people in my childhood neighborhood seemed enthralled by all the new inventions that relieved them of having to do physical work. But those new conveniences (*NEW!* was the big advertising hook of those days) had never given me much satisfaction. Everywhere you looked, people had willfully become more passive—content to let the power mower replace the push mower, to have the dishwasher do the dishes, and to dry the laundry in that new machine rather than use the clothesline in the backyard. TV had begun to lure kids away from playing outdoors. My Quaker parents declined to buy a TV, with all its cowboys and Indians shooting each other, and as an eight-year-old I complained loudly about not being able to watch Hopalong Cassidy in my own home. But now, half a century later, I felt grateful—and lucky—that my play had been mainly outdoors and that as a teenager I had discovered running.

President Kennedy had been far-seeing about the dangers of going soft, but amidst the national traumas of the next few years—the Bay of Pigs, the Cuban Missile Crisis, and the worrisome circling of Sputnik—his call for a fitter population had been swept aside by his more galvanizing call for a rocket ride to the moon. By the time I was out of college, a lot of kids were dreaming of becoming astronauts and sneaking flashlights under the covers at night to read comic books about superheroes and to fantasize about a future of flying cars and robots that would make all physical exertion obsolete. A lot of teenagers rode to school in their souped-up Chevys or Mercs. I guess I'd have done it too, if my parents had let me. For three centuries, until that postwar slack-off, the Americans who had created a revolutionary new society from scratch had been, of necessity, a very tough people. But by 1960, as JFK had surmised, something had changed.

Most of the runners now on this erstwhile National Road were too young to have personally experienced that change. From their first breaths in the 1960s or '70s, they'd lived in a world that pursued the goal of ever greater convenience and speed in all things—fast cars, fast food, fast computers, fast relief from pain, and very fast returns on investment. Most people of their generation hadn't played in the woods and fields much as kids but were amazingly quick with computers and video games. I had read that in the Air Force, the young men who became the top guns at flying fighter jets were the ones who'd been the fastest with video games when they were twelve. (I would also read, years later, about a study at the University of Essex in the UK that found that top-flight gamers "have reactions of pilots but the bodies of 60-year-old chain smokers."[3]) The entire US culture had been hyperstimulated, while, as fitness tests confirmed, legs, hearts, and lungs had weakened. The trouble was, our legs, hearts, and lungs, *as well as* our five senses and fingers, had always been the fundamental means by which the brain connects to the outside world. Our grasp of life, I feared, was becoming disconnected.

In my work at Worldwatch, where I would need to be back

at my desk on Monday morning, I'd seen disturbing data on what that disconnection was doing to the stability of the planet—including the stability of that presumably pristine Appalachian forest we runners would be entering in a few minutes. A quick summary of the work we'd gathered from scientists had suggested that each year, our civilization burned a quantity of carbon-based fuel that it had taken the planet a hundred thousand years to produce. It was no wonder the waste products of industrial metabolism had piled up in the atmosphere just the way they did in the legs of a runner who was going too fast.

■   ■   ■

We were now just half a mile or so from the pass, and there was a lot of shifting of positions and speeds—a restless impatience, despite the steepness of the incline—as we approached the bottleneck. Evidently, it wasn't just I who was feeling that internal tug between the need to conserve energy and the hope of reaching the trailhead before it was choked. The trailhead, where we'd funnel from the thirty-foot-wide National Road to a rocky, single-track path through the woods, was just minutes ahead. I doubted that there was anyone here who wasn't ruefully familiar with the great automotive oxymoron of our high-speed age—"rush hour"—in which the rush slows to a maddening creep.

At the top of the road, just a stone's throw from the trailhead, we would pass the historic Old South Mountain Inn, which in colonial days had been a tavern. If we'd been hiking this course in those more slow-paced last years before the Industrial Revolution, we doubtless would have stopped for a convivial tankard of beer. Not now, though. We were in a race. All my life, it seemed, we'd been in a race—first the arms race, then the race to move up the economic ladder, make money, make waves. It wasn't just rush *hour* that had made us crazy; it was the entire rush *century* we'd grown up in. And this was where one of the advantages I might have in this footrace came most clearly into focus. When humans rush, whether as frantic individuals or as high-powered societies, we are extremely vulnerable to stumbles—and falls. Runners who rush on rocky trails can trip. Corporations— and sometimes entire societies—that get myopically fixated on driving productivity higher at all costs have been known to collapse. President Kennedy knew his history, and he may have had some of those collapses in mind when he wrote his "Soft American" article, in which he observed, "the knowledge that the physical well-being of the nation is an important foundation for the vigor and vitality of all the activities of the nation . . . is as old as Western civilization itself. But it is a knowledge which today, in America, we are in danger of forgetting."[4] Two years later, Kennedy made his challenge to the US Marines. He probably never knew about this first JFK 50 Mile in Boonsboro, which took place in obscurity just months before he died.

I didn't know about that first running either; probably no one but the eleven original participants and a few of their friends or mates did. That was the year I went to work as a teacher at the George School, a private boarding school in Pennsylvania that had hired me to coach the cross-country team and to teach tenth and eleventh graders in the same English department where the novelist James Michener had taught a few years earlier. I was not very competent in the classroom but loved the coaching. I was only a few years older than the kids on the team, ran with them every afternoon, and could not forget that when I'd been a teenager myself, I'd been far more interested in running cross-country than in studying physics or biology, or even the presumably easy subject of civics.

After leaving the George School, frustrated with my cluelessness in the classroom (and sad to part ways with the cross-country kids), I went to work for the Washington, DC think tank where Ted Taylor was doing unsettling research on the nuclear threat. I soon experienced the whole new frustration of knowing that, as an individual, despite my job, I had no more chance than a flyswatter waving at airplanes to help slow the arms race that loomed over us. And then, as I worked with other scientists in other fields, my frustrations only worsened. It wasn't just the deploying of seven thousand nuclear warheads around the world, a lot of them on American mountain ridges like this one, or aimed in this direction, that was insane. The US Congress at that time was trying to pass (with many members resisting) the landmark Clean Water and Clean Air acts of 1972, in the wake of Rachel Carson's revelations in her book *Silent Spring* that the country's air and water were being pervasively poisoned by chemical wastes. As a runner, I could appreciate the importance of being able to breathe clean air and drink clean water and live in a country that was not contaminated by radioactive leaks or chemical dumping, quite aside from being threatened by terrorists driving into our cities with suitcase bombs. So, it wasn't just in the industries of nuclear weapons and power, but in almost every industry our civilization depended on, that we were seeing symptoms of careless shortcutting in the pursuit of quick rewards. To a runner, the idea of taking a shortcut made no sense. In a race, it would be completely self-defeating.

It was then that I'd made that implicit pact with myself: With running, yes, I *would* have some control over long-range outcomes. Maybe I couldn't measurably affect the risks of nuclear catastrophe, or collapsing ecosystems or failed nations, but I could have a measurable influence on the capacity of my own body. I could improve my marathon time. And regardless of what happened to the world, I could become a better survivor. And wasn't that what the evolution of us humans had been all about? Maybe the whole premise of modern society—build a great industrial civilization so that people can live better lives—was backward. Maybe the only way it could work was by building great fitness as individual people, so we can have a more livable civilization.

In the ensuing years, I encountered more specific evidence of how a grasp of our out-of-control *industrial metabolism* (a term first introduced in the 1970s by my physicist brother, Robert) might improve how I manage my *own* metabolism—and an ultrarun could provide the quintessential test. I came across a revealing piece of that evidence in 1991, for example, when I went to work for the sustainable-agriculture pioneer Lester R. Brown, who had founded the Worldwatch Institute, where the Earth Day co-founder Denis Hayes had worked. At Worldwatch, I learned about how past civilizations had often stumbled— and eventually fallen—because, among other failures of foresight, they evidently didn't understand that growing the same crop year after year without allowing the soil to regenerate would cause crop yields to shrivel. A beet crop could exhaust the soil in three years. A patch of Amazon rainforest cleared for grazing could turn to barren desert in five years. The idea that cycles of rest and regeneration are essential to ecological sustenance became a basic part of my perception of life and strongly influenced how I trained in my running.

■ ■ ■

At the top of the pass, we turned off the road just beyond the inn and crossed the flat parking area next to the trailhead.

The level ground provided a welcome relief, and I found myself loosening my shoulders, slowing my breathing a little—getting a moment of respite before hitting the trail. Over the years, I had become aware of how essential it is to grab rest whenever and however you can, whether it's between heartbeats (my resting pulse these days was about forty beats per minute), or in the recovery period between races, or on an easy flat stretch between the hills.

In 1987, I had read in Joe Henderson's "Running Commentary" column that Jim Ryun, who had set the US high school record of 3:55.3 for the one-mile run in 1965, still held that record twenty-two years later. "In fact, no one has broken four minutes in the past 20 years," he wrote.[5] Why not? Henderson, the former editor of *Runner's World*, suggested that the kids in the 1980s were over-raced. In the '50s and '60s, teenage runners would concentrate on just a few major competitions per year—as did Ryun. By the '80s, top runners typically ran several races in a single meet and had major meets scheduled year-round. Henderson's observation was prescient, as Ryun's record would still be standing after *thirty-five* years. Many coaches seemed to have forgotten that fundamental principle of cyclical rest and recovery.

I'd had some early inklings of that principle. In my younger years, when the country's "more is better" approach to consumption was ramping up, some of the hard-core long-distance runners I knew earnestly believed that the more miles you ran per week, the faster you'd run your races. A benchmark for a good marathoner was a hundred miles per week, but one of the guys in the Washington, DC, area was running two hundred miles a week—and, for a while, it seemed to work. For several years, he seemed unbeatable. But then, in 1965, he finished a couple of hundred yards behind me at the Boston Marathon—a bit disconcerting for him, I'm sure. I wasn't in his class. The following year, he made a nice comeback and finished eighth at Boston, but not long after that he must have hung up his shoes. As far as I could determine, his last race was over thirty years ago.

In my exposure to the ecology of agriculture and to the nature of biological processes at large, I found science-based confirmation of what I'd intuitively suspected since my twenties: While stressing the body in training is a key to making it stronger, resting it is equally critical. Adequate rest—and willingness to take days or even weeks off from time to time— is the runner's equivalent of revitalizing soil by letting land lie fallow. Good farmers also knew how to further boost productivity through crop rotation, and here too there was a good runner's equivalent—cross-training. In the 1960s, the term "cross-training" (alternating running with weight training, bicycling, or other complementary exercises) had not yet come into popular use, but experience told me that along with rest, variation of routine was essential to success. During my five years at the George School, I had the kids run very structured workouts most days, but about once a week I assigned them the adventure of simply running somewhere they'd never run before. It would be entirely up to them how far they went, how fast, or where. In today's liability-spooked educational environment that might not fly, but for those boys it did wonders. They'd come back to the campus and tell me with big grins where they'd gone, and sometimes I'd have to stop them and say, "Maybe you shouldn't tell me this." But the various pastures, stream crossings, steep hills, escapes from chasing farmers, and (once) a shirtless dash through the very-off-limits girls' dorm at the school, in a pack, all constituted a form of adventurous cross-training. The muscles got a day off from rigorous pacing, while the spirits (and maybe hormones, as if they needed it) got a lift. For all five years, the team went undefeated in Penn-Jersey conference competition.

By the day of this race, I had been incorporating the paradigms of sustainability into the designs of my workouts for forty years—balancing stress with rest, energy inputs with waste outputs, hydration with perspiration, routine with adventure. When I'd sent in my entry—and asked myself how my years of studying sustainability would help my performance as an endurance athlete—I'd come up with two short answers. The first was that *both are about long-term adaptation*. The kind of "quick study" we were used to seeing in popular storytelling (and maybe expecting in our own lives)—as in the movie *Karate Kid*, in which a few weeks of lessons from the guru transforms the bullied kid into a martial-arts master—is pure fantasy. Reaching the highest possible performance as a runner is a years-long, even lifetime, venture. By the time you get to the starting line, 95 percent of what you'll accomplish in the race has already been done.

The other short answer, as I would soon be rudely reminded, is that *when the trail is treacherous, you have to be able not only to think on your feet but to think with your feet*. As a sentry waved me to the left and into the trail—miraculously clear of the horde that I knew must be right on my heels—I could feel my feet already making unbidden adjustments to the rough ground that lay ahead.

3

APPALACHIAN TRAIL

What Are My Running Shoes For? The
Journey from Barefoot Hunter to "Boots
on the Ground" to Where I Am Now

OVER THE 2,184 miles of the Appalachian Trail between Mt.
Katahdin, Maine, and Springer Mountain, Georgia, there are
about two hundred places where you can leave your car and
make a magical passage on foot from the workaday world to
the wild. It's like entering a cathedral, or a temple, or—for
me—one of those old Quaker meeting houses my parents
took me to when I was a boy. There's nothing about the trail
that immediately announces itself as different from any of
thousands of other trails scattered around the country that
go just a mile or so, or even just a few hundred yards, before
ending in a Walmart parking lot, or the backyard of a new
house, or just a sad heap of beer cans and litter. Yet because
you know this unpresuming path is, in fact, the Appalachian
Trail, you feel a kind of awe.

The Appalachian Mountains are among the oldest ranges
on earth—far older than the Rockies or Sierras or Himalayas.

This ridge we were now running on had been created about four hundred million years ago by the last upheaval of a now quiescent structure geologists call the Short Hill Fault, deep under our feet. Obviously, I thought, the person who came up with the name "Short Hill" had never tried running up South Mountain.

It was a relief to be on the trail, leaving the road for the silence of the forest and the crowd of runners for the single track. With the big climb behind me, I could ease off the hard breathing. But fending off the anaerobic threshold (or *lactate threshold*, as some physiologists prefer to call it) now quickly gave way to dodging rocks and roots. I was glad to be wearing my half-size-too-large Saucony running shoes with their sturdy toe-boxes and cushioned midsoles. In other races, years ago, I'd worn less protective shoes, and too many times had ended up with black toenail. Black toenail is like an inch of the Black Death, just a small reminder that no part of any of us independent Americans is independent of the life-and-death cycles of the earth we run on. I'd been painfully fascinated, in those days, to discover that with the careless kicking of too many rocks, the toenail will hemorrhage, turn purplish black, and a few days later fall off—and then grow back each time like a lizard's tail. It revealed how little I knew about my feet.

Nowadays, with my more protective shoes, I felt more comfortable and confident on the trail—but ambivalent about footwear in general. I needed the protection the shoes provided, but to run well I also needed a good feel for the ground I ran on. Shoes are a kind of last frontier between us and the planet on which we've evolved. They can be conduits of critical information transmitted from earth to brain, through the feet—or they can be impervious barriers. It can be a precarious balance.

I recalled that when I was a kid in the early 1950s, the official Boy Scout handbook advised that hiking should always be done with leather boots or shoes that are high enough to cover the ankles. By my late teens, I discovered how liberating it was to break that rule. The rationale, beyond the protective function of tanned cowhide in the event of a snakebite, was that stiff leather supported the ankles and prevented sprains. But after a few years of cross-country running in high school, I knew that the best protection against sprains was to have strong, flexible ankles and a set of practiced reflexes that let the ankle "give" if it started to turn, the way a skier's knees bend to absorb bumps.

Yet, the Boy Scout rule seemed part of a more general view of man's relation to nature in the twentieth century: You braced yourself with sturdy equipment, rather than learning to bend like a supple tree branch in the wind. In coastal developments, for example, the usual practice was to build concrete sea walls to protect houses from storm surges. But a few years ago, a study reported in the *Journal of Coastal Research* had found that sand dunes provide far better protection than sea walls because they are *not* rigid—they let the water flow around them, slowing it but not standing rigidly against it, because to stand fast is to eventually break. Sooner or later, most sea walls or dikes crack and break.[1]

Until very recently, the US Army and Marines had had their recruits running in boots and not only injuring themselves but learning (in "boot camp") to hate running for life. Even now at the turn of the twenty-first century, most hikers still wore high-top leather shoes. It was all part of the same view that led advertisers of four-wheel-drive vehicles to decide that what sells is to show these vehicles rolling unstoppably through rugged terrain—the same view that had led to the building of the Humvee as a heavyweight replacement for the army jeep. Part of the growing frustration I was feeling at Worldwatch, by now, was that the consumption habits of the general population, instead of being informed by the ecologists and trending toward lighter ecological footprints, seemed to be trending in the opposite direction. Lately, I had begun to see more and more Hummers on public streets.

On the other hand, none of the military guys in this race were running in boots. This race wasn't under the aegis of a giant military-industrial conglomerate; it was being run by highly independent men and women. If you asked the government (or the politicians who spoke for it) how best to strengthen America's foothold in a Darwinian world, the answer was still "boots on the ground." If you asked individuals who were trained to carry their own weight and who had an educated sense of their interdependence with the planet they ran on, the answer was: light running shoes.

A man's relationship with his running shoes, as I was aware, could sometimes be as fraught—even obsessive—as his relationships with women. Maybe by now that was true of female runners, too, although most of the women hadn't yet had as many years to accumulate numerous boxes of running shoes in their closets. In my first two decades of running, I'd seen very few women running (in the 1970 New York Marathon, I think there was only one). But among the guys, I knew at least several who never threw their old running shoes away and by now owned several hundred pairs. A few years ago, I'd gotten rid of a few boxes full of my own by selling them to a guy in Ohio, who happily paid me $5,000 for them. He wanted to start a running shoe museum. I was torn about selling them, but by then I was no babe in the woods; my own relationships with running shoes had run the gamut from romantic to disillusioned.

The romance came first. In my junior year at Westfield

(New Jersey) High School, in 1957, the cross-country runners were issued canvas shoes with thin, hard soles that had no cushioning, no lateral support, and almost no heel—they were what a later generation would call "minimalist." Then I heard about a very different kind of running shoe that all the Olympic runners were wearing, made by an exotic German company called Adidas. You couldn't get them in New Jersey, but I obtained the address of a New York City wholesaler called Carlson Import Shoe Co. that sold them. I took the train to Hoboken and the ferry across the Hudson to the city and found my way to the address—a second-story walk-up in a rundown district that two decades later would be known as Tribeca. Inside, an old man who looked like a character from a Charles Dickens novel peered over his glasses, listened to my request, and brought out the shoes. In contrast to the dull black canvas shoes we'd been given by the high school, these Adidas shoes were bright white with green stripes. They were made of superlight kangaroo skin, and when I put them on I thought I could *leap* like a kangaroo. They were cushioned and felt weightless. I had a magical cross-country season, breaking the school record that had been set by Westfield's state champion Edgar Hoos ten years before. Can a sixteen-year-old be in love? I was in love with my running shoes. And come to think of it, although there'd been hundreds of innovations in athletic footwear engineering in the decades since that time, those magical, cushioned Adidas with their wondrous kangaroo-skin uppers would have been well suited to the terrain I was running on now.

The disillusionment came two decades after the Adidas shoes. In the October 1979 issue of our then two-year-old magazine, *Running Times*, we published the results of a study of 120 models of running shoes that had been conducted for us by a prominent sports podiatrist, Joseph Ellis. As we noted in the accompanying article, "Previous studies have always emphasized laboratory analysis of the materials and design of the shoe. The *Running Times* study emphasizes analysis of the feet and legs wearing the shoe, rather than the shoe itself. This, ultimately, is what the evaluation of a shoe is for: to determine how well the shoe supports the natural motions of the legs and feet—and how well it protects them from injury—during the running motion."[2]

We used ten test runners for the study—five males and five females. The male runners ranged in ability from a ten-minute-per-mile beginner to a world-class competitor (Craig Virgin, who had broken Steve Prefontaine's American record for the 10K just the previous year). The females ranged from a twelve-minute-per-mile beginner to a world-class competitor (Laurie Binder, a national marathon champion and four-time winner of the San Francisco Bay to Breakers race). The runners were wired to test shock (G-force transmitted up the leg to just below the knee) and motion control (behavior of the foot at forty-two equal-time points in the cycle of each step taken). A total of six hundred test runs were recorded.

The study caused a huge ruckus. It had covered the full range of models being marketed to runners and joggers that year, including models that sold for very low prices in mass-market chain stores—knockoffs that looked similar to the shoes serious runners wore, but that if you tried running in them turned out to be bricks. In identifying the results for specific models, however, we just listed the models that tested "very high," "high," or "medium" in the tested qualities. But a number of readers complained that we had not named *all* of the 120 models tested, including the ones that had performed poorly, so in the following issue we went ahead and named them all. And that was when that metabolic by-product we'd been taught in grade school to call "number two" hit the fan.

In the full listings, the very bottom shoe—117th of 120 in shock protection and dead last in motion control—was a model called the "USA Olympics." The name caught our attention because that model was one of the cheap knockoffs that we were pretty sure no Olympic runner would ever wear. Yet, we also knew it was against the law for any commercial product to use the Olympic name without permission of the US Olympic Committee. So, this use (by a giant mass-market chain store) had to be an endorsement! The USA Olympics shoe had a shock reading of more than ten Gs transmitted up the leg—about five times as much as the shoes ranked at the top. We wondered: Would thousands of beginners be injured because they'd been misled by what looked very much like an Olympic Committee endorsement for a shoe that was actually a brick?

Our concern was further elevated when, after our story made the front page of *USA Today*, the chain's national management called a press conference to "refute" our results. To testify to reporters that the USA Olympics was "as good as any shoe on the market," the company had brought a biomechanics expert—a guy we'd never heard of. We did a little investigating of *him* and, after wading through a byzantine web of corporate connections, found that this "expert" was the same man who had designed that model in the first place and was now on the payroll of the chain that was selling it! It was a scandal, and being the eager young journalists (and hard-core runners) that we were, we decided to do an exposé. We were immediately informed that if we did, we'd be sued. We went ahead anyway, with a cover story in the January 1980 issue, "The Great Olympic Shoe Scandal." I coauthored the article with my associate publisher, Jeff Darman, who had been president of the Road Runners Club of America for the previous three years. No one sued. And ever since then, there'd been a general understanding among serious runners: Buy your shoes at a "running store," from a salesperson who is himself or herself an experienced runner. Don't buy cheap knockoffs at a department store, or your feet and knees will regret it.

Of course, that was not the last chapter in the saga of a runner and his shoes. As the number of people participating in road races boomed, the market for good shoes became ever more competitive, and—as had happened with cars—the release of new models of shoes goosed sales and launched a sort of running-shoe arms race. The cheap models were left in the dust, but the serious brands—Adidas, Nike, New Balance, Reebok, Saucony, Lydiard, Etonic, Mizuno, Brooks—sought ways of gaining an edge, and one way was to make the shoes lighter. Elite runners—those rare individuals who had perfect form (no excessive pronation or body weight, etc.) felt they could run faster if they could cut an ounce or two from the weight of their shoes. Manufacturers were happy to accommodate, and "racing" shoes—dropping amidst great fanfare from thirteen ounces to twelve, to ten, to eight, to something called the Nike Sock Racer, which weighed almost nothing at all—became a booming business. I tried a few of them (though not the Sock Racer) and nearly collapsed my arches. By the time I was forty, I knew I'd have to run my races in the same kind of supportive shoes I trained in, probably for the rest of my life. The thirteen-ounce Saucony shoes I was running in for the JFK were the same ones I'd worn in my training runs for the past month.

On the other hand, my diligence with the Sheehan mantra led me to a kind of epiphany about what "listen to your body" really meant. We humans (and maybe other species as well) don't just sense what's happening in our bodies through the mediation of our consciousness up top in the ivory towers of our heads, but also directly through our hearts, groins, skin— and feet. I rationally accepted my need for sturdy shoes, but at a deeper level, I felt a kinship with our ancient predecessors —and maybe it was a yearning not just for more connection with my heredity as a human, but for more direct and intimate connection with the earth on which we had evolved. I didn't believe for a minute that runners were drawn to lightweight shoes only so they could run faster 10Ks or marathons. A big part of it, I suspected, was the genetic memory of how it feels to run barefoot.

■ ■ ■

The trail here reminded me a little of high school and college cross-country. I had always loved trail running in November. The air is exhilarating, and the sky glints through half-bare branches. October has its gorgeous colors, but by November they have turned to something darker, like the bare oak benches in an old meeting house. Even at dawn, you know it is the dusk of the year, when the mysteries of the forest are deepest, the promises most seductive. It is also when the footing is most treacherous. Damp, dead leaves cover the rocks, and in the shadows of the trees those lurking rocks can remain slippery all winter.

My mind began leaping ahead to a section of the AT where, on a training run some years ago, I had taken a bad fall. It was about a quarter-mile long, and I had my own name for it: "Rock Alley." The rocks on that stretch were impossible. And with the passage of the years, I wasn't getting any more agile. I had no particular fear of twisted or sprained ankles, or broken legs, but the prospect of tripping on a rock or root and flying forward—landing hard on my face— haunted me. So common was this concern that when ultrarunners saw blood on a fellow competitor, they knew without asking what happened: "Oh, man, you did a face-plant. Hang in there!" With all the experience I had, this much trepidation felt like a serious failing. I was taught long ago to think positively, to visualize running in harmony. But sometimes, against all the wisdom of the experts, I got visions of disaster instead. It happened when I was driving a car, too—a sudden, mental "flash" of a horrible head-on crash.

I knew I wasn't alone in this preoccupation. If I imagined myself looking back at twenty-first century America from the future, I saw a culture deeply preoccupied with explosions and crashes. Wasn't that what most captivated us in our daily news? If a plane crashed—not just like those four a few weeks ago, but any plane, anywhere in America—it topped the news even if it directly affected no more than a few hundred people, whereas a piece of legislation passed the same day might have life-or-death consequences for a thousand times that many, yet go unmentioned. I know, of course, that the news is selected for its capacity to boost viewer ratings, or entertainment value, more than for its social significance. And this fixation applies equally to the kinds of entertainment that have no pretense of being news. Sitting through a few minutes of previews before a movie, I am subjected to an ear-blasting orgy of exploding cars, buildings, and bodies. And in sports, the moments fans seem to anticipate most are explosive in physical and psychological impact, if not in chemical reaction. During one Super Bowl, a TV commercial for the NASCAR auto-racing circuit highlighted six scenes of car crashes in its thirty seconds of action. This was a putative ad for a racing sport, but in fact it was an ad for a sort of vicarious Roman gladiatorial spectacle, in which—if you watched with any regularity—you might see a car crash with a live driver inside.

In my work at Worldwatch, I had gotten into a somewhat compulsive habit of tracking phenomena that I thought might be clues to what was really happening to us. A couple of weeks ago, after the attack, I had pored through microfilms of the *Washington Post* to see how much space that paper had devoted in the past year to crashes and explosions other than 9/11. While stories about the basketball superstar Michael Jordan (*Had he slowed a step?—Or would he change his mind about retiring?*) had greatly overshadowed news of global warming that year, both of those subjects had been dwarfed by the attention given to various crashes and their aftermaths. We got news of a US submarine crashing into a Japanese fishing boat and sinking it (twelve front-page stories about the crash and its aftermath); racing driver Dale Earnhardt crashing his car and dying; 128 cars crashing in a single, three-mile-long pileup on Interstate 95; a school exploding in China; a Chinese war plane crashing into an American spy plane; an airplane carrying American missionaries crashing in Peru; a truck crashing into a street sweeper; and a Russian plane exploding over the Black Sea, among many others. All told, the *Post*'s coverage for that year, while ignoring most ordinary car crashes, included—as measured in column-inches of text—6,840 inches on crashes and explosions, versus 90 inches on expected impacts of climate change.

The crashes figure didn't include the paper's coverage of 9/11, which had filled the front pages (and many inside pages) ever since the attack. And it only counted physical crashes, although physical instabilities quickly translated into social and economic instabilities as well. The Enron Corporation, a colossus of the energy trade, would soon become the World Trade Center's institutional equivalent. Earlier, when Enron officials were meeting secretly with Vice President Dick Cheney to plan a US energy policy that would open the

Arctic National Wildlife Refuge to oil drilling, the mainstream media had taken no notice. The oil men came and went incognito. But when Enron collapsed, reporters leaped into action and a galvanizing thrill ran through the nation— not a thrill in the joyride sense meant by theme park publicists when they invite us to "experience the thrill" of their newest and fastest rollercoaster, but in the nerve-shocking sense used by nineteenth-century writers describing, say, the experience of stepping on a rattlesnake with bare feet.

As a trail runner on the AT, I had a visceral sense of what that thrill might be about. The Appalachian Trail undulates endlessly when it's not steeply climbing or descending. There are places where you hit a forty- or fifty-foot-long downhill stretch and, instead of putting on the brakes just a little— contracting the quads as you would have to if that stretch went any farther—you just let yourself go. The gravity accelerates you, and by the time you hit the bottom of the dip you're flying as fast as you can without braking or falling, and then the upturn slows you just in time. But while you're still going downhill, if you're flying over rocks, *that's* a bit of a thrill. I suppose it's at least a hint of what kids feel when they jump off cliffs into lakes, or what adults do when they bungee jump or skydive. But the familiarity of that feeling doesn't really explain why it's so seductive. Why would anyone deliberately jump off a cliff and risk dying? Why would I, at age sixty, risk breaking a leg? OK, maybe that question is a little disingenuous, because I can't recall ever hearing of an ultrarunner actually breaking a leg. And I didn't really fear it. In the scores of trail races I'd run over the years—the Pueblo 50 Mile in Arizona, the Pacific Crest Trail Run in California, the Massanutten Mountain Massacre in Virginia, the Western States 100 in the Sierras, the Rattlesnake 50K in West Virginia, and others—I'd never heard of such a thing, except in one high school cross-country race I only read about, which I'll get back to later. I know it has happened, but it must be rare. There's something uncanny about our ability to avoid it, but that too is another story. What I did fear was a face-plant.

About a mile up the trail, a sentry directed us onto that narrow service road—the one that presumably led to an old missile silo. At the top, I scanned the woods, and there it was: another relic, perhaps, of the defensive systems we'd built, whether to protect ourselves from the forces of nature or to fend off forces we've unleashed. All Nike silos, I had read, had long been either abandoned or converted to other uses. But, of course, our leaders were now building newer, more powerful—hopefully less apocalyptic—defenses, fumbling through the same search for balance between security and sustainability as runners choosing footwear for a very treacherous trail.

Here the service road ended and another sentry directed us back onto the trail, which quickly got rougher. Again, I was glad to have my sturdy thirteen-ounce shoes. But it had never left my mind, in the twenty-four years since I'd launched *Running Times* on the third floor of a run-down townhouse in Washington, DC, that our prehistoric ancestors had probably gone their whole lives without shoes. And evidently, our anatomy today was still capable of that. In the third issue of the magazine, in 1977, we published the first of three articles about the Tarahumara natives of Mexico's remote Copper Canyon—a tribe that lived much like our Neolithic ancestors and ran amazing distances over notoriously rough terrain with bare feet. Those native peoples were *literally* more in touch with the earth than we were. Their society was also clearly more sustainable (they had not participated in the escalating of nuclear risks or destabilizing of climate), and I wondered if that was more than just coincidence.

At about nine miles, the trail began dropping down to a pass at Crampton's Gap, where the biggest of the Civil War's South Mountain fights had occurred. The AT hadn't yet been blazed, and I tried to imagine the soldiers in their boots and heavy gear running over these rocks under fire. Men then were lighter and leaner than today's well-fed, gym-buffed guys, but they must have been very tough. I thought of the story of Lawrence of Arabia, whose men lacked the brute force and fortifications of the Turks, but who had the advantage of great physical endurance and mobility—they could walk or run great distances, striking at railroads or forts and then disappearing into the desert. They had won convincingly. Most modern warfare had evolved from the practices of wielding weapons with our arms—spears, swords, longbows, and then guns and artillery, and the controls of tanks or fighter jets—so, not surprisingly, the tools of war are called "arms." But the eighteenth-century French general Maurice de Saxe said the art of war is about legs, not arms. As Lawrence knew, the legs are both the conduit of information transmitted from feet to brain and the main means by which the body makes its way in the world.

If that was true, I was amazed by how little I really knew about my own feet, after all they'd done. For years, I hadn't even known for sure whether to land on the front or back ends of them! I recalled an encounter I'd had thirty-six years ago when I ran my first marathon—the Cherry Tree Marathon in New York City, several years before the first New York Marathon—that had changed my relationship with my feet forever. I'd been competing in long-distance races for ten years at that point and had always run the way my high school cross-country coach had taught—on my toes, or the front halves of my feet. "Run on your toes!" the coach shouted the first time he saw me run. It felt awkward when I tried it (my natural tendency was to land on my heels), but he pointed out to me that that was what the school's fastest 100-yard and 220-yard sprinters (who were also the star running backs on our football team) did, so I accepted that that's what I should do, too.

At about seventeen miles into that first marathon, I found myself catching up with a man I knew to be a legend in the New York running community—Ted Corbitt. Ted had run the marathon for the US in the 1952 Olympics and had been the national champion in 1954. He'd also been the founding president of the New York Road Runners Club and third president of the Road Runners Club of America. He was older now and not as fast as he'd once been, but I could hardly believe I was catching him. As I pulled alongside, Ted glanced at my feet and smiled, and said, "You know, you might run easier if you let yourself land on your heels." It was as if I'd been spoken to by God. I took what he said to heart, and over the next several months, I let myself gradually return to the way I'd landed on my feet before that first day of cross-country in high school. My feet, ankles, legs, and back all became more relaxed, and ever since that day, I had felt more in touch—well, I *was* more in touch—with the ground I was running on. Years later, I would surmise that Ted Corbitt's quiet suggestion had added twenty years to my running longevity.

A few years after this JFK, I would hear about a study that found that over a four-year span, Harvard University cross-country runners who landed on their heels had higher rates of injury than those who landed on their forefeet—the very opposite of what my own experience had suggested. The result seemed counterintuitive, because in short events, from 100 meters to the mile or even 5,000 meters, where most top runners do land on their forefeet, the greater speed and longer strides required for those races requires greater biomechanical force, which puts greater stress on the legs and feet. In the slower, longer distance events, more of us land on our heels—exerting less force, and therefore presumably making ourselves *less* vulnerable to injury than we'd be if we ran like sprinters or 800-meter runners.

The Harvard study seemed to belie my Ted Corbitt epiphany, but I thought I might have an explanation. The study's results were for cross-country, which is run at neither very short (primarily forefoot) nor very long (primarily heel-strike) distances. At the college level, the races are run at in-between distances, around 10,000 meters, where both heel strikers and forefoot strikers can be competitive—and of course both were represented on the Harvard teams. But the training for cross-country requires a lot of interval work or other high-speed running. Those of the Harvard runners who were naturally inclined to run on their heels may therefore have been farther out of their element—pushing the envelope, biomechanically—than were the natural forefoot strikers. The stresses on feet and knees were therefore relatively greater for the heel strikers than for their forefoot-striking teammates, so their vulnerability to injury *at these speeds* was greater. If the same groups of runners had been training for marathons or ultras, with much less speed work but greater mileage, it would have been the forefoot strikers who were more out of their element—and the injury results would probably have been reversed.

That explanation might beg the question of why long-distance runners shouldn't take advantage of the greater power that can be deployed by running on their forefeet, just as sprinters or milers (or about a third of the Harvard cross-country runners) do. The answer was suggested by *another* study of the heel-versus-forefoot question (reported by David

Carrier, the University of Utah persistence-running theorist), which found that while heel striking is slower, it is about 53 percent *more energy efficient* than running on the forefeet. In short-distance footraces, just as in short-distance car races, energy efficiency offers no advantage in performance. If a drag-race driver knew he had the fastest car, it wouldn't matter to him if the car were so energy-squandering that it got only two miles to the gallon. Only its power and speed would matter. Similarly, if a sprinter or 800-meter runner gets only two-thirds the distance per one hundred calories of fuel that a heel striker gets, it doesn't matter. But for an ultra-distance runner, it matters hugely. Sprinters have to run on their forefeet to maximize their power. Most ultrarunners land on their heels to maximize their *staying* power. I had been a successful cross-country runner in high school and college, but at the Cherry Tree Marathon, in my first attempt at a much longer distance, I was a prime candidate to learn how much more easily I could run this distance—and eventually run even farther—by reducing the force of my foot plant. Ted Corbitt, who a few years earlier had been the best ultrarunner in the country, knew that at a glance.

Now, just short of ten miles into the JFK, touching down on my heels helped me keep my footing on the loose stones as I came down the hill into Crampton's Gap. I passed the aid station without stopping and headed back up the other side of the pass, bracing myself psychologically for the rocky six-mile haul to Weverton Cliff.

4

WEVERTON CLIFF

The Art of Breathing and the Music
of Motion: Do My Feet Have Eyes of
Their Own?

TWO HOURS EARLIER, as we ran single-file up the trail from
the National Road, there'd been a lot of that peculiar trail
runner's practice of carrying on conversation with the person
right behind you—like what a not-fully-attentive bus driver
might do with a garrulous passenger in the seat directly behind him. At the same time, though, like the bus driver
watching out for a suddenly braking car ahead, you have to
take care not to step on the heels of the runner just in front
of you. I'd once inadvertently stepped on the heel of my
main rival in a two-mile college track championship just before passing him on the last turn and going on to win by a
couple of seconds, and while his shoe didn't come off, I felt
guilty about it ever after.

By now, though, the field had stretched out so far that in
some places I couldn't see anyone ahead, and we were starting to feel the effort, so the chatting had stopped. I liked the

silence. But there was also something disquieting about the leafy quiet of these woods. Nothing was visibly wrong, but I knew from my work at Worldwatch that the world's forest cover—including large swaths of this very ecosystem—was disappearing at a rate that in evolutionary time is just a blink of the eye. I wondered, *Will my grandchildren be able to run in these woods?*

I knew that soon, thank God, we would begin the descent to Weverton. It was a relief being *able* to know that—and not just a relief but, from an evolutionary standpoint, a gift. If measured not in brute power or speed but in ability to adapt to the enormous complexity of the physical world, we biped walkers and runners are still far more advanced than the sometimes catastrophically flawed systems of military security, food security, or communications security we've built. Humans, thanks to several million years of biological debugging, can anticipate the moments ahead—the trail ahead—in ways none of our inventions can. Our aircraft may be able to carry us hundreds of times faster than our legs can, but the planes can't plan their own journeys. We are still their controllers.

The AT here was up-and-down—no more big-hill climbing, since we were now on the spine of South Mountain, but a lot of smaller hills of a few hundred feet as the ridge undulated. I was breathing harder on these stretches, but also knew that over the years I'd learned to use breathing to gain competitive advantage, the way a Tour de France bicyclist would use his gears. A racing bike's gears are more limited than the runner's limitless repertoire—indeed, *all* human technologies are still relatively crude simplifications of what evolution took thousands of centuries to perfect—but the principle is the same. One of our most basic adaptations, in our journey through the millennia, has been to get *as much distance per breath* as we comfortably can. On some of the downhills, I fell into a spontaneous pattern of six strides per breath. Interestingly, five of the six steps would coast me through a single exhalation, in five little pumps in synch with the steps, followed by a single big in-breath:

> *Out-out-out-out-out, In,*
> *Out-out-out-out-out, In,*

and so on, six steps for each full breath out and in. Then, as the downhill ended and the path swung back up, I needed more oxygen and shifted from a five-to-one to a two-to-one ratio:

> *Out-out, In,*
> *Out-out, In.*

But of course, the undulations of the trail were not at all like a theme-park rollercoaster, where our modern engineers have made every circuit exactly the same. To begin with, this wasn't a ride! But more important, the trail was endlessly irregular, no ten feet of it the same as any another. It was like life itself—no two ten-minute spans ever exactly the same. The runner has to adapt to continuous new experiences. And being at my best on the irregular terrain of the trail called for subtle adaptations of breathing. I might find that five-to-one downhill pattern shifting instead to one in which, while the exhalation still stretched over five steps, the inhalation broke into two quick intakes on a single step:

> *Out-out-out-out-out, InIn,*

like something a drummer might do—two quick taps on a single beat. That breathing pattern would instantly change the stride-to-breath ratio from five-to-one to two-and-a-half-to-one with no break in the rhythm—something dictated perhaps by an abrupt momentary change of terrain (jumping a log or a gully) that can be achieved without any interruption of optimal oxygen flow. For a guy like me who didn't have great leg speed (I'd *never* had great leg speed, even at my peak), the hills and gullies might give me a chance to compete on a more level field (so to speak!) with guys who could always outrun me on flat ground. I thought of Bernd Heinrich, who had set new standards for over-forty-year-olds by running record-breaking fifty-mile and 100-kilometer races on flat courses in Chicago two decades ago. Bernd had to be right around my age. If he were here today, would I have a chance?

A mischievous fantasy came to me: What if, around the next bend in this trail I should suddenly, up ahead, catch a glimpse of Bernd Heinrich? I was pretty sure he still ran. A tiny wave of adrenaline raced through me. How ironic would that be? A few years back, I had come to believe that the most defining attributes of humans are not the power and speed we've achieved with our technologies, but the endurance and patience—and capacity for *envisioning the path ahead*—that had enabled our evolution as persistence hunters. Heinrich was the guy who had started my mind down this "envisioning" path to begin with. Now here I was, not *exactly* envisioning, but *imagining* envisioning . . . and then imagining *seeing* (him, from behind). And it was all based on a memory of first reading (another form of imagining?) what had been written by, and later talking on the phone with (a kind of surrogate seeing?), the guy I was imagining envisioning and then seeing, ahead of me. The brain had come a long and tortuous way on the evolutionary trail, since the time of *Homo erectus*, or *ergaster*, or whoever they were who had survived all the dangers and found their way to where we were now. Who *were* those guys? Now, for the briefest moment, I identified with Butch Cassidy and the Sundance Kid. How many hominid hunters had had to be sacrificed to hungry lions or rampaging boars before it all got worked out? The brain was a living, amazing, Rube Goldberg machine! And yet, for all its powers, it was incredibly vulnerable to misfiring; there were hundreds of millions of confused people on this planet whose imaginations had leaked into what they were seeing, or who saw only what they wanted to see, or who remembered what had never happened, because it was what they had once envisioned. And for all its complexity, the brain was curiously limited, as well. I couldn't *quite* envision Bernd Heinrich because I didn't know what colors he'd be wearing, or what his running form looked like. (When I'd coached high-school cross-country decades ago, I'd discovered that I could look across a space of two or three hundred yards and recognize any one of the kids on the team just by his running form, as surely as if I were seeing his face.) So, this fantasy was conceptual, not visual. And even conceptually, it was only a fleeting shadow of a fantasy in any case, because, on a logical level, I knew Bernd *couldn't* be up ahead. He hadn't been in the final list of entrants, which I had studied on the race web site. It was possible that by now he had retired from competition. I knew there were about fifty men in the age sixty to sixty-nine division in this race, but since the climb to South Mountain, I hadn't seen any of them.

In any case, I knew Bernd Heinrich lived in Vermont, so although his greatest runs had been on flat ground he probably had ample experience running on mountains. And I wouldn't be surprised if he had long ago become at least as conscious of his breathing as I was. I had the impression, though, that most runners took breathing more or less for granted. It was autonomic—you didn't *have* to think about it. If the trail took you to a steeper grade, the strides-to-breath ratio shifted without your being conscious of it at all. As the evolutionary biologist Dennis Bramble was already confirming in his research at the University of Utah, and as I well knew, variable breathing patterns come naturally to the human animal whether you pay attention to them or not.

For me, though, the act of breathing on the run was *no longer always autonomic.* In learning about aerobic metabolism, I had taken at least two bites from the apple of knowledge since those innocent days of high school and college cross-country. The first occurred when I reviewed an article my younger brother, Alex, wrote for *Running Times* in 1982, about the impact of aerobic running on the human brain. He approached the subject with an academic's curiosity, summarizing the findings of more than a hundred studies that had been done on the effects of physical exercise on mental capacity. Not surprisingly, the studies yielded intriguing evidence that aerobic exercise, in particular, correlated strongly with improved capacity for cognitive activity, memory, and judgment. "The world's most valuable natural resource is not gold, or oil, or uranium," the article began, "It's *oxygen.*" It continued, "Ancient peoples believed that breath contained not only the secret of life, but the secret of the soul. 'God formed man of the dust of the ground,' the Old Testament tells us, '*and breathed into his nostrils the breath of life, and man became a living soul.*'"[1]

A few paragraphs later, I came upon one of those observations that made me wonder how something so obvious could come as such an epiphany. "The same circulatory system is responsible for transporting oxygen to both the muscles and the brain," Alex wrote. "This . . . makes body and mind *inseparable.*"[2] He went on to cite a wide range of studies in which performances on mental tests of all kinds, under all sorts of conditions, had improved significantly with aerobic exercise. Math students, people with low IQs, artists who relied on highly stimulated imaginations, and senile patients in a VA hospital—all showed remarkable physical *and* mental improvements when oxygen delivery was increased. It strongly corroborated what President Kennedy had argued in his call for Americans to get serious about getting fit.

My second bite of this knowledge came as a result of my work with environmental scientists and their analyses of what they called the "carrying capacity" of the earth. This work would later be encapsulated by the concept of the "ecological footprint"—the idea that each living person uses a quantifiable amount of the earth's air, water, land, and biological productivity to get through life. One day, when I was pondering what that really meant, it struck me that a person who achieves a smaller footprint doesn't just use less, but also gets more out of what he or she uses. "Resource efficiency," you might call it. For a long-distance runner, a smaller footprint meant not only not trashing the trail, the way an all-terrain vehicle would; it meant more ground covered per breath of air taken.

It took me a while to grasp the full significance of that. When we published our first articles on the Tarahumara, in 1977, our interest in the subject was more about the adventure than the science. Alex, who had just joined us as a senior editor, contacted a man named Jonathan Cassel, who had trekked into Mexico's remote Sierra Madre and spent several months living with one of the last of our planet's "primitive" tribes—a people for whom running long distances over some of the earth's most forbidding terrain was not only a principal means of sustenance, but the heart of their social and spiritual life. I think what Cassel told us may have been our first introduction to the concept of persistence hunting. When Alex asked Cassel, "Why *do* the Tarahumara run?" Cassel explained, "It's a matter of survival. If they don't run, they don't eat." He described the Tarahumara territory: the vast reaches of the Barranca del Cobre, a meandering canyon as big as the Grand Canyon and two thousand feet deeper. "There's no cover and concealment in the territory, and without that you can't have much animal or bird life. High up on the plateaus, there are some rabbits. A few wild turkeys, but not plentiful. You have no firearms . . . so when they spot a deer or a wild turkey, they run that particular animal or bird down."[3]

"Running down a wild turkey sounds like an impossible feat," Cassel mused. "[But] the bird is heavy, and after a flight he tires very quickly and must land, and by the time he lands the Tarahumara are almost there. He takes off again, and three or four of these takeoffs and he's too tired to get off the ground and they kill him with a rock."[4]

That year, we published three articles about the Tarahumara, all based on interviews with Cassel. In May 1984, we published a fourth article on the tribe, by John Annerino, recounting the adventure of Annerino's wilderness-running friend Dave Ganci. I don't know whether either Annerino or Ganci was aware of what Cassel had done seven years earlier, but Annerino wrote, of Ganci, "He wanted to be the first Arizonian, if not *chavochi* (white man) to run with a Tarahumara." At five feet, ten inches, and 157 pounds, Ganci was "built very much like a Tarahumara Indian," and he was tough. He made his way to the rim of the Barranco del Cobre (Copper Canyon), and after an arduous trek he found a Tarahumara who could be a translator for him and another (a man Ganci estimated to be in his late fifties), who agreed to run with Ganci from the bottom of the canyon back to the rim, a distance of about twenty-five miles up an unrelenting, treacherous incline. The two natives ran lightly ahead, barefoot, repeatedly getting far ahead but then slowing to let Ganci catch up. A mile from the top, Ganci found himself getting dizzy, took a bad fall, and was knocked unconscious—he must have hit his head on a rock. He was carried to the rim by the two Tarahumara, who were shy and polite when he regained his senses, but couldn't hide being somewhat amused by the whole experience. Then, while Ganci lay contemplating the nature of his existence, the Indians said good-bye and started the run back down to wherever it was they lived—bringing their outing to a total of fifty miles on rocks, without running shoes, water bottles, or a single day of planning.[5]

Annerino's story was fascinating and entertaining, but only seemed to deepen the mystery of men (and women, and children) going ultra-distances *not* as exceptional individuals of their kind, but just as people doing what *everyone* of their tribe does. Since the Tarahumara's "kind" is the same as our kind, whoever or wherever we may be, this sort of phenomenon was bound, sooner or later, to attract the interest of anthropological and evolutionary scientists.

In August 1984, three months after we published Annerino's article, the first scientist to articulate what we now know as the "running man" theory of human evolution published an article in the journal *Current Anthropology* titled "The Energetic Paradox of Human Running and Hominid Evolution."[6] The author was David Carrier, a graduate student of the University of Utah biologist Dennis Bramble. At the time, the idea was given little credence by academics, who argued that running ability could hardly have been an advantage for early humans on the Darwinian field of battle, when other animals were so much faster and more powerful. But

Carrier was lucky; instead of being thrown to the academic wolves by Dr. Bramble, he eventually convinced Bramble that the persistence-hunting hypothesis made sense.[7]

I lifted my eyes briefly off the ground ahead to look around at the ancient ridge I was traversing and tried to imagine chasing a wild turkey. Would the bird be accommodating enough to follow the trail, so I'd at least have a chance, rather than fly off across the rubble of the ridge? Even with that half-second of looking away, I stumbled; I caught my balance but knew there was no way I could run over this ground if there were no trail. And the Sierra del Cobre might be even rougher, though the rocks there wouldn't be hidden by leaves. It would involve far steeper climbs, of the sort that can make even a highly trained runner feel the bear on his back. Or maybe in Copper Canyon the metaphor for anaerobic distress should be a *mountain lion* on your back.

What Alex and I—and apparently Jonathan Cassel and John Annerino, too—had not thought to ask, in any of our articles, was that most fundamental of questions: How do the *Tarahumara* breathe? How do they run up higher-than-Grand-Canyon walls so easily? Or more specifically, how do they get oxygen from the air to their muscles—and get rid of metabolic waste—with such extraordinary efficiency? It was a question we hadn't ever really examined in our own running, either. Like most other runners we knew, we assumed optimal breathing just came naturally. As naturally as breathing!

The only advice I'd ever heard regarding how runners should breathe was offered by a yoga guru I once read about, who stated that runners should breathe only through the nose. I restrained an impulse to tell him, "I'd like to see you get off your mat and try it!" To take in the sheer volume of air needed to run any faster than a slow walk, you have to open your mouth. And granted, that's *not* something that requires instruction. Joan Benoit recalled a similarly funny experience some years ago after her Olympic Marathon victory in 1984. When she was in junior high school, she tested in the ninety-fourth percentile for fitness, according to the criteria used by the President's Council on Physical Fitness and Sports. "The teachers told me my rating would be higher if I knew how to breathe properly while running," she wrote in her book *Running Tide*. "I got the last laugh on that score." In the Olympic Marathon, she said, she breathed the same way she had in junior high.[8]

But while our magazine staff didn't ask questions about breathing, the Utah scientists David Carrier and Dennis Bramble did. In their research comparing the anatomical features of mammals that are primarily walkers with those that are built for running, they eventually made a highly revealing discovery: While quadrupeds like antelope, horses, or cats are locked into a pattern of respiration that allows just one stride per breath, we two-legged creatures are anatomically capable of taking two or three or more strides per breath—just as I'd been doing on this trail. Years later, Bramble's explanation of this phenomenon would be misquoted in a popular book, in a garbled passage suggesting that we humans are great endurance runners because we can take multiple *breaths* per *stride* (allowing us to "pant to our heart's content," as the author wrote)—the very opposite of what Bramble had actually found and of what I thought any experienced runner must know.[9] Yet, no one seemed to notice (in any of the reviews or blogs I read) the garbled description of how we breathe. Was I somehow misconstruing what I'd read? I contacted Bramble, describing some of my own multiple-*strides*-per-*breath* patterns and asking if he'd been misquoted. He replied that he had. "The runners we tested ran exactly as you describe," he wrote to me.[10] I could only conclude that the reason for the book's many readers not questioning the quote was that most runners do, indeed, assume that their breathing is autonomic and that no questions need to be asked.

In the years before this JFK, the main thing I knew about quadruped running was that animals that didn't have bare skin, and that couldn't sweat the way humans did, would more easily overheat. That had been a central hypothesis of the running-man theory: The persistence hunter chased the animal over the hot African savanna until it became overheated and had to stop. And if the animal was big, with a higher volume-to-surface ratio than we skinny humans have, it would overheat even faster. I had not yet heard about Bramble's observation that humans have more flexible patterns of respirations than quadrupeds. But as I shifted from the road-racing of my twenties to primarily mountain trail running in my middle years, I became more conscious that on irregular terrain my breathing was not at all regular, and that its variability might offer the opportunity for deliberate improvements in the delivery of oxygen to the muscles. There were plenty of physiological precedents: Someone who is panicking may hyperventilate, but if persuaded may also be able to deliberately slow his respiration. People who practiced meditation were known to be able to deliberately slow their heart rates. And neuroscientists had even begun to demonstrate how someone with a prosthetic limb could actually move it by deliberately *thinking* about moving it. What we had assumed to be biological limits could be transcended more than I'd ever dreamed. It seemed clear to me, then, that to get the greatest possible distance per unit of oxygen taken in, I needed to listen, not just to my body in the general sense suggested by the Sheehan mantra, but to my *breathing*, and get a feel for the efficiency of the various patterns I was hearing, because learning to interpret that biofeedback would gradually—perhaps over months—help me go *farther per breath* as I became more practiced.

So, right there was that second sweet bite of the apple of metabolic edification. The inhalation of oxygen might be a given—a gift to all who are alive, whether awake, asleep, or oblivious—but it is also, beyond that, an art by which that gift can be made greater. I began noticing, as I ran on the trails near my home in Virginia (and occasionally chased a deer for a few seconds until it got smart and left the trail), that as I listened to my breathing I was also playing songs in my head— classic rock from the 1960s and '70s, mostly, but sometimes tunes I couldn't identify or perhaps was making up as I ran. I wondered if the long, rhythmic runs of the persistence hunters might have played a role in the origins of chanting, or singing, or even of music itself. In 1982, a writer at Oxford University Press, Herbert Mann, had sent us an article revealing that Mozart had done a fair amount of running in his day and had even participated in at least three races (in the fifteen to twenty kilometer range) near his native Salzburg, Austria. Not knowing quite what to make of this revelation, we published the article with this teaser at the top of the page:

> Scholarly research reveals that Wolfgang Amadeus Mozart, the little-known runner who competed in several road races in 18th-century Austria, was also an accomplished musician.[11]

Nineteen years later, in preparation for this JFK 50 Mile, I was running up a particularly steep hill on the Blue Ridge of Virginia and heard myself gear down like a mountain bike rider, from a two-to-one to a one-to-one stride-to-breath ratio (rare for me, except on a steep climb), with an audible emphasis on the *out* breath:

Out, In,
Out, In,

and the sound I was hearing was:

Hoo, hah,
Hoo, hah,

and then it struck me that what I was hearing was uncannily like what I would hear from a group of highly oxygenated US Marines getting psyched for the start of the Marine Marathon or Army Ten Mile—or the start of the JFK 50 Mile, just two hours ago:

Ooh-rah!

■   ■   ■

At around thirteen miles, I found myself suddenly on that dangerous stretch I'd been obsessing about, Rock Alley. I was hyperalert here, focused mainly on the ground four or five strides ahead, and once again thankful that I could focus there and not on the ground immediately underfoot where the next few steps would land. Once, in another race, I'd heard a runner just ahead of me on a stretch of outrageously rocky trail exclaim, "Do my feet have eyes of their own?"

It would be natural to assume, in this age of remote-controlled war planes and Google, that the kind of automatic guidance of the feet that bypasses conscious decision-making, while impressive, can't compare with the capacities of some of the twenty-first century technologies we've built. But a few months ago, at a meeting of the Foundation for the Future in

Seattle, I'd heard the physicist Michio Kaku say something quite to the contrary: that even if Moore's Law of expanding computer processing speed held up, it would be the year 2049 before machine capacity caught up with that of the fully deployed human brain. Civilization had now come to a very rocky path. I was glad I didn't have to depend on electronic guidance systems to run this last segment of the AT. It was hugely empowering to know that if I was good at this, I could not just think on my feet but think *with* my feet. Maybe, in retrospect, that feeling of empowerment was just a bit too hubristic.

I made it about three-quarters of the way down the switchbacks of Weverton. The AT is usually a good path, but on this stretch it snakes through a true boulder field. Every step of the way, you have to rely on that quicker-than-consciousness mapping of the protruding rocks and roots with unwavering focus. You might come up behind a runner who is moving more slowly and call out "passing on your left," but just the distraction of glancing at him as you move by momentarily joggles your subconscious calculation of the height of a rock. The sole of your shoe scrapes the rock instead of clearing by a quarter-inch and you lose balance and lunge awkwardly for a second, but recover.

Just a few hundred yards from the bottom, though, a rock that wasn't supposed to be there hit the toe-box of my shoe— just a quarter-inch more than a scraping, but enough to stop my foot in its track while the rest of me flew forward and down in a full face-plant on more rocks. Actually, when such an event occurs, the human body is so remarkably programmed that the face almost never hits the ground; it is the knees, followed by elbows, forearms, wrists, and both of the hands, that fly forward in the head's defense. I remained prostrate for a shocked second or two, and the next runner behind me stopped. He didn't have to, but it's what ultrarunners almost always do.

"Are you OK?"

"I'm OK, thanks." I had no idea whether I really was, but it would have been unbearable to me to be out of the race. The guy took off toward those cheering voices. I got to my feet and followed slowly, blood trickling down my leg and arms. A few minutes later, coming out into the sunshine, I got a terrific cheer from the crowd.

5

KEEP TRYST ROAD

With a Little Help from Our Friends:
The Not-So-Loneliness of the Long-
Distance Runner

IF THE JFK ultra has a midlife crisis, this is where it begins. Just minutes ago, you felt your mojo at its peak, flying down off the mountain into Weverton and arriving at the aid station to raucous cheers. Looking back, though, it's almost like you'd been racing through an endless hotel corridor and burst mistakenly into the wrong room—a big celebration of some kind—in your shorts, all bloody and sweaty, and your socks and hair festooned with dead leaves and dirt. Where on earth did a trail ultra come up with *spectators*? But it was no mistake. The crowd formed a big, friendly gauntlet—hands reaching out to offer water, banana, gels, electrolyte drink. You paused briefly to take whatever aid you needed, and in seconds you were back into the trees running a half-mile section of wooded trail that took you under a highway bridge to another sunlit place where you're about to cross a railroad track, and reach—at last, thank God—the C&O Canal

Towpath. Weverton still echoes in your head, but it's like a flicker of dream that's fading quickly.

You are about to begin a twenty-six-mile-long stretch of flat, turf/gravel path—the real test, because you no longer have the hazards of the Appalachian Trail to give you focus and keep you in the moment. You've already been running for over two and a half hours—about the time it takes a very good runner to do a marathon, except that the rocky trail has burned up a lot more energy than a marathon, so you no longer have much glycogen left in your legs or liver. Your body has played athlete since dawn, and you've succeeded in not crashing (well, there was that rock that reached up and grabbed my foot a few minutes back, but that's not the kind of out-of-fuel crashing I fear most).

I have always struggled with anxiety, maybe more than most people do, and as soon as the fear of falling was behind me a new anxiety hit: Where was my crew? I'd expected to see my wife Sharon and daughter Elizabeth in the crowd at the bottom of the descent, so I'd passed up the aid tables there in favor of my own electrolyte drink, which Sharon would have ready (I didn't trust the commercial ones, which contained refined sugars and chemicals). But then suddenly I found myself back in the woods on the link trail to the towpath without having seen her—and with my bottle still empty. How stupid was that? There was another place where spectators gathered at the end of this next half-mile, though. *Maybe* . . . and then, there they were. I refilled my bottle and gave Sharon a kiss. It was just a few seconds, but a kiss from my wife, and the realization that I really couldn't run this race without her support, was one of those moments on which the long hours of the race rested. The stop took less than a minute, but seemed to give me as much lift as a half-hour's worth of glycogen. I gave her and Elizabeth an appreciative smile and headed back into the race. And then almost immediately, I was hit by another anxiety: I'd forgotten to ask about the competition. Had they seen any other guys my age go by ahead of me?

But then, of course, how would they know? At the gym in Boonsboro, before the start, there had been a hundred guys who looked like they might be in their sixties—balding, gray beards, creased faces. A lot looked like the pictures I'd seen of nineteenth-century prospectors or trappers, and not at all like the too-well-fed, smooth-faced politicians and celebrities our age that you'd see on TV. And the older guys at the start looked as fit as the young ones, just more weathered or craggy. I'd seen Frank Probst and a few others I could identify from races I'd run over the years. But most of the older guys I didn't recognize. I knew from the entry list that they were from all over the country. No way could Sharon know if I'm the first one through here or not. In any case, I needed to shrug off my anxiety and my competitiveness; at just sixteen miles into a fifty-mile race, it was bad medicine.

At the little open area where Sharon and Elizabeth were waiting, a cracked asphalt road comes to a dead end at the old Chesapeake & Ohio Railroad track that runs along the canal, with the Potomac River visible just beyond. This is Keep Tryst Road, which we had scouted yesterday with the car. Maybe in part because of its name, it reminded me of other dead-end roads I'd come across in my past life, where teenagers would park on summer nights and make out. We called them "lovers' lanes." Even before I was a teen, I knew of a few such roads. In those days my family didn't have TV, and nobody had video games or other virtual worlds. Our world was the outdoors, which offered adventure aplenty. The first time I ever witnessed a sex act was not in an X-rated movie or video, but peering through the window of a car I came across one afternoon at the end of my street in Berkeley Heights, which at that time dead-ended in the woods. I was probably eight (a fairly innocent age in those days), and it felt as if I'd stumbled on something profoundly forbidden.

I would eventually learn, as I grew older, that the "forbidden" in my country—and probably in most countries—is almost synonymous with the unknown or the poorly understood. Before the journeys of Leif Eriksson and Christopher Columbus, the unknown regions of the Atlantic Ocean were, for European seafarers, a forbidden realm. Worldwide, people of different cultures shared a nearly universal abhorrence or fear of exploration that went too far— whether by a Galileo probing the solar system in violation of church dogma or a young couple exploring new mysteries in a car, out of their elders' sight. One of the fundamental appeals of an ultra is that it *is* a venture into the unknown. Can you withstand having your heart race not just for the twenty seconds of an exciting action-movie chase, but for eight straight hours? When you sign up for an ultra (or any long-distance footrace, now), you sign a legal waiver of any claims should anything go wrong. If a train was approaching as you reached the track here, and you rushed to beat it and got killed, it was your choice.

I had felt a bit of unwanted tension on that half-mile link trail from Weverton, because the railroad here is still active, and if a train comes along, you have no choice but to stop and wait. In a foot race, having to stop and wait feels awful, like having a really good dream interrupted, and if you're trying to run for a record, it feels like disaster. The company that owns the trains, CSX, is a corporate giant too big even to recognize the *existence* of something like a trail race, say nothing of adjust its schedule to let the race cross its track unimpeded once a year. Mike Spinnler, the race director, had asked, but to CSX his request had apparently been like asking American Airlines to please not fly any planes over suburban Maryland on Saturday afternoon because you're having a pool party. They declined, and when Spinnler then asked if they could at least tell him just *when* the train would go through on the third Saturday of November each year, so he could alert the runners, he apparently didn't get an answer to that either. (Years later, they would relent.) I'd heard that some years a train would pass Keep Tryst Road at a point when maybe the first two hundred runners had crossed the tracks and the next hundred would have to stop and cool their heels. For runners chasing age-group records, it *was* a disaster (what if the guy you have to beat barely makes it across just before the train, and you're fifty feet behind him, catching up, and have to stop? Or what if you've run your heart out building a ten-minute lead over a rival, and he runs at a more relaxed pace and catches you standing there just as the last box car crawls past?) And these trains didn't just take a minute or two to go by; they were long-haul freight trains moving at around eight miles an hour and sometimes pulling a hundred cars.

One reason the trains here moved so slowly, I'd found, is that the track goes through a narrow, curving tunnel that was cut through the rock along the Maryland shore of the Potomac for the Chesapeake and Ohio (C&O) Railroad in the 1870s. In my recent cogitations about the history of technology, I'd stumbled on an unlikely connection with this very railroad. One of the characters I most vividly recalled from my boyhood was the folksong hero John Henry, who wielded his rock pick in a race with the new jackhammer that had been brought to the rock-breaking business by the Industrial Revolution. I've never been a Luddite, but I liked the spirit of John Henry—his unwillingness to let his strength be usurped by a machine. I didn't know *where* John Henry was supposed to have done his feat—until I came I across an intriguing bit of research. Scott Nelson, an associate professor of history at the College of William and Mary, found evidence that after the end of the Civil War an inmate in a Virginia prison named John William Henry had been rented out by his warden to work on the C&O railway, and it was this John Henry who was the basis of the legend. What particularly struck me, in view of what I'd been thinking about the lethal nature of an American economy in which technologies were rapidly supplanting our own bodies and minds, was what Nelson had written about the way the workers who dug those tunnels endured such punishing work: They "managed their labor by setting a stint, or pace, for it. Men who violated the stint were shunned."[1] The workers had a song that told "*what happened to men who worked too fast:* their entrails fell to the ground. You sang the song slowly, you worked slowly, you guarded your life, or you died."[2]

Luckily, this year, no train was in sight as I reached Keep Tryst; I quickly crossed the track and came to the T at the famous C&O Canal Towpath—a flat gravel-and-dirt path that runs parallel to the canal along the Maryland bank of the Potomac River for 184 miles from Washington, DC, to Cumberland, used by mules pulling the canal barges in the nineteenth century. At the T—a momentous intersection for any runner in this race, but especially for me—I paused. Here I would turn right, but first I had to take a thoughtful look left.

The war between North and South, despite the fact that its ghosts were all around us here, seemed a faint schoolbook memory. I had a personal link to that war, though, and it was hard to pass this intersection without thinking of it. A few miles south across the river was the village of Waterford, Virginia, a Quaker town that proved to be a virtual no-man's-land during the war. In the 1860s, the town's postmaster, John

Dutton, had three daughters who were unusually independent for those times; they published a fiercely pro-Union
newspaper, the *Waterford News*, that lectured on the evil of slav-
ery, and they distributed copies to both sides. The sisters, who
were twenty-six, twenty-four, and nineteen years old when the
war came to their town, also had the chutzpa to declare in
their paper that Waterford was a war-free zone—a century
before Berkeley!—and that any soldiers of either side entering their town would be required to check their weapons. I
loved it! That didn't exactly work out, however, and the rebels
did considerable damage to the town. Given Waterford's
proximity to the bloody battles of Manassas and Bull Run, and
the girls' anti-Confederate provocations, the Duttons were
fortunate not to have their house burned down (it's still there,
in good shape). After the war, the youngest sister, Lida, mar-
ried a Union cavalry officer, John Hutchinson, who then became a Quaker himself. Their great-grandchild, Alice
Hutchinson, turned out to be my long-distance-swimming,
bicycle-riding, organic-gardening mother.

■ ■ ■

Also to the left somewhere was the spot where Bobby Kennedy had finished his own fifty-mile hike on a wintry day four
decades ago—one of the first of the thousands of Americans
who responded to his brother's challenge to the Marines.
That unexpected response, not just of Marines but of civilian
men, women, and kids all over the country—then dubbed
the great "fifty-mile craze" of 1962—had begun its gestation
when JFK wrote his "Soft American" article, arguing that a
high level of physical fitness was essential to the kind of intel-
lectual strength and civil resilience the country now needed,
in what was proving to be an era of unprecedented dangers.

In the winter of 1962–63, John Kennedy came across an executive order that was written half a century earlier by another president who valued physical vigor and had been similarly concerned. In 1908, Teddy Roosevelt declared that all US Marines should be able to prove their fitness by walking fifty miles in three days, doing the last half-mile by alternating two hundred yards of double-time marching and thirty seconds of rest, then sprinting the final two hundred yards. The records showed that some of TR's officers had done the distance in *one* day, and Kennedy wondered whether the Marines of 1963 were as fit as those of 1908.

On February 5, 1963, the White House put out a press release about the Roosevelt order, noting that the president had suggested to General Shoup that he find out how well his Marines could do, compared with Teddy Roosevelt's Marines. A group of officers was called up to do the test. However, JFK's brother, Bobby, who was the nation's attorney general, decided he was going to do it too, and wasn't going to wait for the Marines. That Sunday, Bobby set out on his hike. The weather was freezing, the towpath was covered with slush, and one by one the aides all dropped out. As the last one quit at mile thirty-five, Bobby commented to him, "You're lucky your brother isn't president of the United States." Kennedy reached fifty miles in 17 hours, 50 minutes.

Within days after Bobby Kennedy completed his hike (there's a photo of him looking uncharacteristically exhausted and having his feet massaged by his wife, Ethel), thousands of civilians likewise responded to the challenge intended for Marine officers. A fifteen-year-old, Paul Kiczek, did the distance and decades later revisited the experience in an Internet search of 1963 newspaper stories about the hikes. He found that a New Jersey paper, *The Daily Record*, reported on February 15, 1963, that a twenty-four-year-old policeman and ex-Marine, Francis Wulff, had done the feat on the spur of the moment. "I read about some army officers shooting off their mouths about the Marines and I decided to give it a try," Wulff told the reporter.[3] On February 16, the same paper reported that a group of eight teenagers from Boonton, New Jersey, had set out in subfreezing weather, and three had gone the distance. One of them, seventeen-year-old Ken Middleton, remarkably finished the fifty miles in under twelve hours—which meant he had to have run a good part of the distance. On February 22, the paper reported that The Mansion House Tavern, in Boonton, had announced a competition, a "Fifty-Mile Endurance Walk" to take place on March 10, with a $25 Savings Bond for the winner and free draft beer for everyone who finished. Meanwhile, in Marin County, California, four hundred high school students set out to do the fifty miles, presumably even without the incentive of free beer, and ninety-seven of them finished.

Needless to say, not everyone who tried the fifty miles shared Bobby Kennedy's mojo. JFK's overweight press secretary, Pierre Salinger, hiked six miles and called it a day, commenting, "I may be plucky, but I'm not stupid." He told reporters that if he were to attempt fifty miles, the result would be "disastrous."[4] In Butler, New Jersey (again, from *The Daily Record*), two high schoolers who had neglected to get their parents' permission to be out past the town's curfew got stopped by police after just three miles. And in Washington, DC, William Kendall, an aide to Republican Congressman Peter Frelinghuysen Jr. walked just five miles, which he apparently considered quite enough to prove that Republicans, unlike impulsive Democrats, walk "for a purpose." (Maybe this was the origin of the proliferation of AIDS walks, breast-cancer walks, and other fund-raisers that helped to deflect social costs from taxpayers half a century later.) Kendall explained, "We did not set some hopelessly unattainable goal such as Pierre Salinger did. We had an objective . . . whereas the Democrats strike out aimlessly with no objective. When they get worn out, somebody picks them up in a truck."[5]

Across the country, the fifty-mile fad was met with quick scorn and skepticism from medical and health experts. From the American Medical Association: "People can endanger themselves. We get distressed when people go out and strain themselves."[6]

From the National Recreation Association: "The 50-mile hike verges on insanity."[7]

From the Soviet Union's Olympic track coach: "So a man walks 50 miles in one day—what of it? Tomorrow he catches a taxicab again to go four blocks."[8]

And from folk singer Phil Ochs, a sardonic song that poked seriocomic fun at an American population he depicted as so chair- or couch-bound that a lot of people never even got their feet on the ground. Unlike the don't-strain-your-heart American Medical Association, or the enjoy-the-view-from-your-Airstream National Recreation Association, Ochs—who called his song "Fifty-Mile Hike"—took delight in suggesting that it was high time for people to "get in step" with the Kennedy challenge.

So what was Kennedy thinking? Did he have second thoughts about the assertion he'd made in his "Soft American" article, that the need was not necessarily to train our youth to be warriors, as the Spartans did, but to achieve something more fundamental to a nation's long-term survival? One clue may be that, unlike some of the politicians who would succeed him, Kennedy had an abiding interest in military history and in the rises and falls of empires. He probably wasn't just thinking about the physical endurance of the Marines, but about a broader set of concerns: the roles of persistence as well as power, of patience as a reality check to sudden urgency, and of the long view as an essential factor in planning, especially in response to emergencies. I wonder if he sensed, even before its outlines were clear, that the world was headed toward a global emergency even more all-encompassing—and fateful—than that of the global war that had ended a few years earlier. Scientists had not yet clearly foreseen the specter of catastrophic climate change, and the threats of ecological failure, resource wars, peak oil, and Malthusian outcomes were then only faint shadows on the horizon. Whatever JFK had in mind, he never got to fully explain it in a thoughtful memoir, or even in policy discussions, given his life's abrupt end the following year. But his call was taken to heart by more than the just the Marines.

■　■　■

If this was in fact near the spot where Bobby Kennedy had finished his walk, it was also the juncture where now, four decades later, several contingents of Marines and a whole army of civilians—people who had chosen to take what Robert Frost had called the road "less traveled by"—would once again carry on. Or, *were already doing so.* As I made the turn to the right, I could see a fairly long distance up the path toward Harpers Ferry, and I couldn't see any Marines coming back to me. I felt an urge to pick up the pace but was also beginning to feel some fatigue. Conflicting internal signals vied for attention. Away from the noise of Weverton and Keep Tryst, I was once again aware of that tension between the peaceful surroundings and the violent secrets they held. Now that tension was back at the front of my consciousness, if only because my outsized fear of rocks had been temporarily pushed aside.

6

TOWPATH

Learning from Quarterbacks: The Slower-Is-Faster Phenomenon

GOING FROM KNEE-BUSTING single-track trail to a wide, flat, lightly graveled turf was a relief. I figured I was still ahead of about 850 of the runners, and now I could lengthen my stride without fear of falling. And because the towpath was about ten feet wide, there was no problem with passing—no need to call out "passing on your left," then hope you didn't fall on your face as you veered off the edge of the trail into a quick detour over a minefield of rocks hidden under undisturbed leaves.

It was turning out to be a beautiful day, with bright sunlight sparkling on the river, which I could glimpse through the trees a couple of stones' throws to the left. Now and then, I passed a couple of Saturday bicyclists or walkers, and because they could see only one or two runners at a time—we were now stretched out for miles—they probably had no idea they were sharing the path with the largest ultrarun in the country. Sometimes large events go unrecognized, if only because our vision is so focused on what's immediately around us that we are unaware of the bigger picture. I recalled the evening in 1990 when the mayor of New York City, Ed Koch, put on a banquet at a fancy midtown hotel to mark the twentieth anniversary of the first New York Marathon, and some of us original participants were invited up to the podium to share a few memories. We particularly recalled that most of the people we ran past in Central Park apparently had no idea there was a race going on. One of the guys recounted how he'd passed what he thought was an aid station and grabbed a piece of fruit, and then was startled to find himself being chased by a shouting fruit vendor. And of course, the runner grabbing the fruit had been as focused on the race as the people he passed were unaware of it. To see everything that's happening around you is not easy.

Apparently a lot of long-distance runners remember incidents like that. Clarence DeMar, after winning his seventh Boston Marathon, recalled that a man who saw him running down the road one day in the 1920s took pity on him (maybe thinking he looked like a guy running in his underwear, who might be in some kind of trouble) and tried to give him a dime so he could at least afford to ride home on the trolley.

We runners regard marathons as very big events, but recalling those stories reminded me, with amusement and pain, of how sometimes even *really* big events, like the changing of the earth's climate, go unnoticed. If a ninety-year-old visitor to Glacier National Park were to comment that all the big glaciers he'd seen there as a boy were now less than half the size they'd been when he was young, his grandchildren might doubt his memory—or he might even doubt it himself. We mortals forget so easily, because we're trapped in the moment of our own time. But as I'd been discovering, at least since my first introduction to the evolutionary scientists' persistence-hunting theory of human origins, endurance running can put us in closer touch with our long-term past—and, maybe by extension, even with our long-term future. The key is to escape from that mental box of our own frantic moment.

I was jerked from my reverie by the sight of a young Marine about fifty yards ahead of me suddenly lurching off the path and throwing his arms around a big beech tree, dry heaving. I felt for him; I've done my share of dry heaving in races, and it's wretched. I had hoped some of the Marines would come back to me, but not *this* way. I didn't say anything encouraging to him as I passed and would later hate myself for my silence. Maybe he'd been too aggressive in the early going, but that's something an athlete can learn only through hard experience.

That lesson is hard because it's not just a matter of pacing. It's also a matter of calming the turbulence in our heads and chests, which throws us out of rhythm, poisons our blood, and burns energy too fast. The causes of that turbulence are omnipresent in today's world, and unless you're a Buddhist monk or a still-practicing Quaker, you can't avoid them. Ironically, I thought, one of the most pervasive causes was that everything in our culture seemed to have turned into a race—a race to invent, bring to market, build wealth. A race to win, in a culture where if you don't win, you lose. And here I was in another race. I knew I wasn't the only runner out here who was feeling too much tension. But then again, one of the reasons a lot of us *were* runners was to blow off stress.

Of course, our tension had heightened since September 11th, but like the wisdom of George Sheehan's "listen to your body," the weight of that tension was a thing that everyone acknowledged but few examined very closely—possibly because we were resigned to it. We might be outraged about the terrorist attacks, but we were resigned to the pervasive stress that had long predated those attacks. Even before the planes struck that morning, almost no American questioned it: If you wanted to succeed, or even just survive, you had to move fast. Next year, it would have to be faster. And after that?

My brother Bob's wife, Leslie, worked as a programmer on the giant Univac 1 supercomputer in the early 1960s, and it was mind-boggling to everyone how fast the Univac could do a thousand or even a million calculations. One day, not long before this race, I asked Leslie how long it would take that car-sized machine to do a *trillion* calculations. She recalled the machine's speed, then we figured that if it had been run day and night, and kept from overheating, a trillion calculations would have taken about fifteen years. Yet, the day would come when Intel Corporation would unveil a chip the size of a fingernail that would do a trillion calculations in *one second*. The acceleration was a tsunami that engulfed every aspect of our life, so how could anyone fight it? Or, for that matter, how could anyone not *celebrate* it? So, while we agreed that we were hopelessly stressed out, this new power to do everything faster was irresistibly seductive.

Our parents' and grandparents' generations believed that the rewards of life come from years of hard work, but we were conditioned—by commercial advertising and the promises of politicians—to want those rewards *now:* the winning lottery ticket, the lawsuit award, the casino jackpot, the racetrack win, the guy from that "you may already have won" contest coming to our door with a check for ten million dollars— and, soon, the clever day trade, the lucrative initial public offering, the merger, the flipped house, the illicit Nigerian fortune. We'd become a nation of impatient two-year-olds! Horatio Alger was dead; Bill Gates was king. And then seduction morphed into addiction: We were *addicted* to ever greater speeds and to the enormous and ever-increasing power necessary to keep up.

That was what almost everyone understood and acknowledged, and almost no one resisted. It was a primrose path. But the picture I'd gotten from my work with Ted Taylor, not so long after the jolting inception of this acceleration at Hiroshima, and now from my work at Worldwatch, was different. And what I understood *as an endurance runner* was different—in a way that provoked not just rumination in my head, but tension in my shoulders and turmoil in my gut.

I passed the first of the twenty-six concrete mile posts I'd see along the left edge of the towpath between here and Dam Number 4. This one had a big "59" painted into indented numerals, that being the number of miles this was from the starting point of the towpath in Washington, where the C&O Canal coming from the west and Rock Creek from the north both emptied into the Potomac—at the "water gate" for which a nearby hotel of now notorious repute was named. The next post would be number 60, which would be seventeen miles into the race. The dam, a little under four hours from now if all went well, would be about half a mile past post 84.

What I learned from Ted Taylor was a brutally simple reality, but one to which most people either had not yet been exposed or just could not believe: that we no longer had control of the technologies we had created. I love movies but thought it intriguing how wrong the sci-fi movie *2001: A Space Odyssey* had been. This *was* 2001, after all—yet what had actually happened by now was far from what the director Stanley Kubrick had envisioned. At the same time, the movie was prescient in ways he probably never imagined. Since the end of Kennedy's Apollo program and the canceling of the Orion Nuclear Propulsion program (a plan to build the next generation of spaceships powered by controlled nuclear detonations, which Taylor had been chosen to head, but which was later ruled to be in violation of the 1963 treaty banning nuclear detonations in outer space), the US manned space travel program had halted. And Hal, the famous Univac-sized usurper of human volition, had not appeared and probably never would. We humans are still the bosses of our technologies, still fully responsible for any unintended consequences of their use. Those consequences weren't Hal's doing, but our own.

A spectral figure appeared in my peripheral vision. It was Frank Probst, my erstwhile age-group rival, slowly passing me on the right. This year we were in different age divisions, as he was still fifty-seven, but I didn't like being passed by him—especially the way he looked now. Frank is tall and looks a lot like the actor Ed Harris, but today his head was tilted to the side like the top of a broken corn stalk bent over by a strong wind. Yet, the weather this morning, at least so far, was as innocent as it had seemed that morning when he was nearly obliterated by the plane that hit the Pentagon. He glanced at me as he pulled even and mumbled something about not having completely recovered from . . . and then he was past me, looking awful with his oddly cocked head, but nonetheless leaving me behind. I was too tense.

In the 1970s I realized that it wasn't just the nuclear industry that was out of control—and causing a tension in me that even now, after all these years and all my experience as a runner, I still had trouble fighting off. Ted Taylor wasn't working alone but had formed a partnership with my brother Bob and a group of research assistants who were profoundly concerned about the human future; they were part of a new breed known as *futurists*. They called their group International Research & Technology (IR&T), opened an office on

Connecticut Avenue in Washington, and wrote a mission statement inspired by the work of Rachel Carson and others who grasped the dangers of technological hubris. Hiroshima had been not only horrifying but—to many—secretly thrilling, because it ended the war in a flash. After the agonizing duration of campaigns like the month-long ordeal at Iwo Jima, the one-second defeat of Japan had been a revelation. Our destiny, most Americans would assume henceforth, was to keep expanding power and speed in all things.

The futurists were running scared, as were the environmental scientists I would work with years later at the Worldwatch Institute. The consensus of these scientists was that, in sheer magnitude, the coming impacts of global warming, most traumatically in the intensification of storm surges on coastal cities, could be to Hiroshima what Hiroshima had been to a gunshot. By now, global warming was widely acknowledged by climate scientists to be unstoppable. It could be *mitigated*—slowed—if the governments of the world grasped its urgency, but the US and other key governments owed their elections to entrenched interests that didn't want to see that happen. Whatever urgency the environmental and climate scientists felt, I felt too—maybe even more so because I felt helpless to help them. In America, power and speed had become a virtual religion, impervious to arguments about unintended consequences. The proof of this new faith's hegemony was that it did not bother to challenge or compete with any established religions—it simply swallowed them without their knowing it. Only the Amish, and perhaps a few Quakers and Buddhists and Unitarian Universalists, seemed to have any serious reservations.

As the race continued, I was now approaching an old iron trestle where the railroad left the Maryland embankment and crossed the river. I glanced to the right, across the canal—

long stretches of it now dried up and overgrown by weeds and saplings. I was reminded of what I'd learned about the root causes of our civilizational acceleration. Both the canal and the railroad had begun construction the same year, 1828, both built to haul coal for the new technologies of the Industrial Revolution. Coal, which enormously escalated the power of humans to dig, lift, pump, haul, smelt, forge, illuminate, communicate, and make tools, was the beginning. It was joined a few decades later by its fossil-fuel cousin, oil, the first commercial oil well having been drilled a day's carriage ride north of here, in Titusville, Pennsylvania. But while coal was dirtier and more polluting (possibly the most Brobdingnagian oxymoron of the entire modern era is the advertising slogan "clean coal"), it has remained the godfather of fossil fuels to this day. The C&O Railroad won the race for transportation dominance along the Potomac corridor because it was powered by coal, while the canal's barges were powered only by mules.

The difference was big enough to be ultimately world-breaking—and fairly revealing about why I was here, in this spot, at this moment. Looking across at that trestle, I could hear myself paraphrasing the Humphrey Bogart character Rick in *Casablanca*: Of all the fateful forks in the road of the human journey, in all the millennia, why here, why now? This trestle wasn't any recognized monument of that journey—not an Acropolis or Western Wall, or even a Kitty Hawk or Cape Canaveral. But it was the very spot where two fatefully different conceptions of what I can only call "earthly metabolism"—the energy-use fundamental to all life—had parted ways. Off to the left had gone the railroad, ten times as fast as the mule but burning fuel at a hundred thousand times the rate that the mule was. Straight ahead had been the path of the mule. The mule ate no more in a year than an amount of oats or hay that could be grown in a year on that one mule's share of the earth. The train had won the race, but at what might well be apocalyptic cost.

How so? The Carboniferous period, which produced that coal, lasted sixty million years, and if our civilization should end up consuming (let's say) about half of the planet's fossil energy over a span of three centuries (nineteenth through twenty-first), before it's either too uneconomical or too dangerous to extract more, we will have used one hundred thousand years' worth of photosynthetic production for each year we lived during those three centuries. It struck me that the *real* forbidden fruit, when humans began their transition from Eden to the kind of knowledge that corrupts, was not an apple but a lump of coal.

So, the metabolic parting of ways represented by this trestle wasn't just unsustainable; it marked a moment in evolutionary history that, if your whole life took place within it, might have seemed "normal" even though *inside* that evolutionary moment the speed of events was escalating astronomically. The story of the Intel chip was being replicated in every area of life—in the production of energy to do the work our bodies had evolved to do, and in the production of products we don't really need.

As a runner, I now understood that, in metabolic terms, civilization had gone into a dead sprint. What was *oxygen debt* for a human runner was *resource depletion* for the human economy. What could be a run of no more than one or two minutes before a gasping, hands-on-knees halt for a sprinter, versus many hours for an endurance runner, was equivalent to a civilizational run of a few decades, versus centuries or millennia to come. We were living in a sprint economy. At first, I thought of it as an intriguing parallel; later, I grasped that it was more than that.

One of the first scientists to see a significant parallel between the human body and the industrial economy was Henry A. Bent, a professor of physical chemistry at North Carolina State University, best known for his landmark 1971 article in the journal *Chemistry*, "Haste Makes Waste: Pollution and Entropy." In 1978, Bent wrote:

> Exhaustion of muscle cells' high-energy phosphate reserves by strenuous exercise, like exhaustion of a planet's oil reserves by fast living, requires (after 20 seconds or so for the human body) a further decrease in the system's power output.[1]

Bent wrote this just a few years after the US lower forty-eight reached peak oil production in 1973 (it has been in steady decline ever since), triggering intense discussion among energy experts about how long it would be before we reached the inevitable *global* peak. Some were forecasting that it would be reached around 2012, although we'd then need several more years of data before we'd know for sure that the peak had in fact been passed. And some believed that once that confirmation came, if alternative energy was not yet fully ready to take over from oil, global chaos would ensue.

So, now I knew that when the railroad had split off from the canal and crossed the river, right here at this trestle, it wasn't only the new king of American industry that had taken a road never before traveled. The train was an early leader of a global race that, at its current pace of consumption and waste, couldn't possibly be sustained. It was like that clueless guy who sprinted the first half-mile of the Boston Marathon only to crash minutes later. And meanwhile, it was generating turmoil in anyone who sensed what was happening—or at least in me.

High-level athletes have found a way of conjuring calm in the storm, and when they apply it they can sometimes achieve extraordinary, even astonishing, performances. It is a skill they describe as "slowing the game."

In the years leading up to the 2001 JFK, I started to notice a significant link between the time perception of an endurance athlete and that of a sustainable civilization: *If you want to go as fast as you can, don't rush!* It's a genuine paradox, and on a basic, athletic level coaches explain it as pacing. In physiological terms, there's no mystery: If you go too fast, metabolic waste products can pile up in your legs and lungs and force you to a halt. Or you can use up your glycogen before you reach the finish and be forced to rely on frustratingly slow-burning fat—or, worse (if you are stubborn enough to keep going) be forced into cannibalizing the protein in your leg muscles. Of course, in an athletic event lasting only an hour or two, you can also go too slow and end up realizing that you still have energy left. (A football or soccer coach, after witnessing a great performance, will sometimes talk approvingly about how an athlete "left it all on the field.") The goal is to find that sweet spot between exhausting your fuel too soon and having something left. In an ultra lasting many hours, however, there's unlikely to be anything left, other than excruciatingly slow-burning fat. The main risk is running out of usable energy too soon.

On another level, however, the don't-rush paradox can be hard to grasp and harness. Experienced athletes know not only to seek the physiological sweet spot but to seek the somewhat more elusive condition in which all systems are working in complete physical and emotional harmony—

where everything *feels* right. In sports talk, it's the "zone." It happens, for example, when two evenly matched basketball teams meet and one of them goes on a run of eighteen points during which the other team scores zero. "We were in the zone," say the guys who did the run and then won. Asked to explain what happens to allow that, the athletes often speak of everything "slowing down."

By getting their mental and physical systems into synch, athletes heighten the capacity of their senses to seize the moment and own it. If you're a baseball player at bat watching a fastball approach at ninety-seven miles per hour, or a football quarterback trying to track your receivers amidst the mayhem of colliding bodies, you need to slow the scene perceptually in order to take control of it. If you're a cop on the side of the road and a driver speeds past, the driver will be a blur, but if you pursue and pull alongside, matching your speed to his, you'll see him almost as clearly as in a still photo. For the athlete, meshing mental perception with the physical scene unfolding is like matching the cop's car to that of the speeder—speeding up the perception to slow down the scene. A guide for high-level quarterbacks at the Alamo City Quarterback Camp in Texas explains: "As the quarterback gets more and more reps [practice repetitions], the picture he sees will become clearer and clearer . . . and the opponent's movement seems to slow down while the quarterback's speeds up."[2] Athletes and coaches in a wide range of sports have alluded to this paradox:

> "He is at the point in this game that the game
> has slowed down for him."
>
> —Green Bay Packers coach Mike McCarthy,
> referring to quarterback Aaron Rodgers after
> Rodgers led the Packers to victory in the 2011
> Super Bowl[3]

"[English soccer star] George Best and former basketball player Michael Jordan are among those to have remarked on how time seemed to slow down when they were 'in the zone.'"
—Steve Taylor, author of *Making Time*[4]

"Great athletes . . . say the game 'slows down' for them, particularly at critical moments. That's why a baseball player or tennis player can read the spin of a baseball or tennis ball when it looks like a blur to the rest of us. . . . The fastest way to your goal isn't always fast."
—Roy S. Johnson, Editor-in-Chief, *Men's Fitness*[5]

For me, in a slow-twitch event that didn't demand lightning reflexes (except maybe when I was running downhill over rocks), the need wasn't so much to slow down a blur of motion *around me* as to slow down the commotion *inside.* I am as prone to anxiety as I am to falling, and too often in my competitive life I've found myself racing another runner as if we were in the last mile instead of in the middle of the race with many miles yet to go. Now, in my anxiety, I was running too turbulently within myself, like the industries of the sprint economy in my larger world. And just as that larger world can move toward a far longer-thriving existence if it can adopt more of the attitudes of slow food, meditation, carefully considered decisions, and what Buddhists call mindful living, I would ultimately run this race *faster* if I could *slow down!*

7

ANTIETAM AQUEDUCT

Redemption: A Recovering Strength
for the Human Runner—and for the
Human Race

ANYONE WHO DREAMS of one day running the JFK should be
cautioned about the weather. And with climate scientists now
preparing us for a time of intensified weather events, it's true
of *any* extended outdoor adventure. If a Santa Ana wind in
Southern California could flip eighteen-wheelers over on
their sides, as was happening more often now, you can imagine what it might do to a long-distance bicycle race like the
popular Tour de California. Cross-country skiers have to be
alert to anomalous snow-melt, hikers to high-water stream
crossings, farmers and gardeners to untimely budding in
mid-winter. In the years to come, the weather will be more
and more in our face.

The JFK 50 Mile, though, had a weather history that predated our awareness of human-caused climate disruption.
The first race was held on March 30, 1963, eight months before JFK's assassination. The next twelve runs were also held

in the spring, but spring weather in the western Maryland hills can be brutal. The 1974 race was hit by a late-winter storm so devastating that a majority of the entrants were unable to finish, knocked out by hypothermia, frostbite, the pleadings of frozen support crews, and existential questioning about what in the world they were doing there.

Race organizers subsequently moved the race to November, but the tradeoff was that November brings a chill wind down the Potomac, and when you emerge from the relatively sheltering forest of the Appalachian Trail at Weverton and start up the towpath, more often than not you'll hit a cold headwind. It might happen the moment you make the right turn at Keep Tryst and then pound you for the whole twenty-six miles to Dam Number 4, or it might just smack you with gusts.

This time around, the weather was kind. Given my hope of breaking the age-division record, I felt lucky. There'd been no noticeable headwind as I turned onto the towpath. Somewhere north of Harpers Ferry, though, I came around a long bend—I think they call it Dargan Bend—and the wind was suddenly there like a cold hand pushing against my chest. I was trying to run north; the wind wanted to push me south. What I felt was in no sense a complaint—difficult wind comes with the territory, and many ultrarunners *revel* in difficulty. The more impossible the conditions, the more they love the challenge. But it threw an elemental new anxiety into my run.

It's a curious thing, how the weather outside our skins can so powerfully evoke our emotions. In the literature of the human journey, weather is an omnipresent metaphor, a periodic reminder of how absolutely linked we are to our world. The physical tension of running against the wind was almost literally a slap in the face; it attuned me to other, deeper, tensions I was now feeling. It struck me that a big part of the push-and-pull this course had on me was the sense of unresolved questions it confronted me with—and they weren't trivial questions, but true matters of life and death.

First, there was the lingering presence of a war that had been fought all along this course over grievances that had never been entirely resolved, even by now, two or three generations later; yet, the space occupied by that haunting presence was simultaneously occupied by crowds of friendly, life-loving descendants from both sides. I knew perfectly well that the conflicting economic and social views that had torn the country in the 1860s still tore at us now—the details different, but the divisions still present. In my own lifetime, I'd seen the manifestations—in the civil-rights conflicts that raged during my college years, a century after Lincoln's Emancipation Proclamation and punctuated by the assassination of Martin Luther King Jr. in that tumultuous year of 1968. It was the year when I fled from teaching to run road races in the Bronx and Yonkers and study exercise physiology at Columbia—the year I found myself wondering how we could know so much about the body and so little about our own minds. I'd seen the rifts again in the Vietnam War protests . . . and then, in just the past nine weeks, in the tense debate about whether the nation's response to 9/11 should properly be outright revenge or something that might require a tougher, less impulsive, and more far-seeing stance.

Just a few miles up the towpath, I would come to Antietam, where the contradiction in the air would be most acute. Antietam Battlefield was the site of the bloodiest single day in the military history of our country, but when I got there a big crowd of friends and spectators in a festive mood would welcome me. I knew, from what I'd experienced at Weverton, that what I passed through at Antietam would be nothing less than a celebration of life at its very best, as we were living it right now, by descendants not only of the armies that had fought there, but also of the more ancient humans who'd gone out on hunting excursions together—hunting game and not other humans. As far as I knew, no primates or other mammals in their natural state mounted massive warfare against their own species.

Up ahead, I could still see Frank Probst, his head askew like a fire hydrant that had been hit by a truck. I had always been a good judge of running form, and if I hadn't known Frank's running as well as I did, I'd have sworn he was in trouble and was coming back to me. But I knew, from past encounters, that Frank would be a lot harder to catch than he looked. I recalled, with chagrin, the time a few years ago when we had done the Bull Run Run, a fifty miler in northern Virginia, and around halfway through the race I spotted Frank up ahead of me looking very much like an old man on his last legs. I passed him easily, going up a short hill, and said something friendly to him as I went by. A couple of hours later, I hit the wall, stopped at an aid station exhausted, and sat down to gather myself for the final ten miles. As I sat there, old Frank came staggering by, *still* looking like he was on his last legs. After a minute or two I got to my feet and went after him, but never caught up. This time, I knew better. He might look slow, but this was a guy who nine weeks ago had dodged a 757.

Frank Probst also represented an enigma that had been a part of my fascination with this race as long as I'd known of it—the relationship between war and sport. Both were about physical competition—about striving for dominance or victory. At least historically, both had been about men trained to defeat other men by means of superior physical fitness and martial skill. I wondered if one of the roots of JFK's vision of a strong nation—though he publicly denied it—really had been the model of ancient Sparta, which trained its young men to be warriors from boyhood. In modern America, sports coaches often employed the language and skills of military officers or drill sergeants. Nazi bombing raids on London were called the Blitz, and so are football tacklers' attacks on a quarterback. Both warriors and athletes, at least in modern spectator sports, put great emphasis on the wielding of power and speed to prevail.

And yet, for all these similarities, the differences between sport and war were as large as life and death—and in my mind *were* about life and death. How could these two realms, each engaging millions of men and women with intense dedication, be so closely allied and yet so opposite in their effects? That question added another dimension to my competition with Probst. Frank was the old soldier in running shoes. I was the old Quaker in running shoes. The question still remained: What was the connection? It must have been another of those tensions kicked up by the cold wind off the Potomac. In a couple of miles, we'd reach that hallowed place, and for the spectators there—and for Frank and me as well—it would be only a day of sport, with no trace of the rage that had once swept across the land.

■   ■   ■

A possible explanation for the strange connection between sport and war was suggested by the Claremont College anthropologist Paul Shepard, who noted that while hominid hunters benefited from cooperation within the hunting party, they also survived and evolved through competition with other groups. If our species was going to win out over the lions and hyenas in the long run, we had to have not only that critical advantage in our evolving ability to envision dinner around a bend, but the shorter-term advantage of using that ability in competition with our fellow hominids. Competitiveness in the Darwinian sense had to be very much in our blood as we moved from hanging out around the fruits and nuts to chasing the mammoth. But with the advent of civilization, wrote Shepard, some of that inborn drive to prevail in the hunt may have been frustrated and redirected in ways that have had tragic consequences.

Shepard surmised that the advent of agriculture, which allowed one man to produce enough food for ten or twenty, meant that most men no longer had to hunt, or—in a world of fixed settlements and guarded territories—even *could* hunt. Yet the hunting instincts continued to be activated by our DNA as generations of boys became men. Shepard theorized that that instinct, stymied by a lack of actual hunting opportunity (we now had domesticated cattle, sheep, goats, chickens, and pigs we could kill without chasing), was transmogrified into an appetite for hunting other *men*—transforming us from hunters to warriors.

Shepard's discussion of the agricultural revolution echoed much of what I learned from Lester Brown at Worldwatch—and then heard further articulated by virtually all of the pioneers of the environmental movement. Agriculture—the domestication of plants and animals—had made it possible for people to live in permanent settlements and not have to wander the earth in search of food, and those settlements had given rise to cities and new occupations and civilization. But they had also separated people from the environments they had become adapted to over hundreds of millennia. That separation, Shepard suggested, had played havoc with long-established patterns of human behavior. In addition to resulting in ecological monstrosities such as soil-depleting crops, it had short-circuited the long-evolved mental wiring of many men.

"War is the state's expression of social pathology," Shepard wrote in his book *The Tender Carnivore and the Sacred Game.* "Ecologically, it is a breakdown in the distinction that a healthy species makes between inter-species and intra-species behavior, and in the use of organized predation. It occurs where men cannot regularly hunt and where population densities are too high. In a Frankensteinian fashion, it fuses elements of the primate rank-order system with the cooperative yet lethal talents of the human social carnivore."[1]

Shepard was suggesting, in effect, that war is a consequence of separation from our origins. I wasn't very knowledgeable about the Bible, but it seemed to me from what I recalled of the Quaker Sunday school I attended as a kid that that was also the story of Adam and Eve being cast out of the garden of Eden. The ultimate separation from the creation is hell. And of course, war is hell. A species that has experienced virtually endless war over the past ten thousand years is, more than anything else, a species that has become separated from its origins and lost its way.

"Cut off from hunting reindeer, horse, and elephant, men lost both the models and means by which personal integrity was achieved and measured within the group by peaceful means," Shepard wrote. "They found a substitute in the biggest and most dangerous potential prey remaining—men themselves. . . . The collapse of an ecology that kept men scarce and attuned to the mystery and diversity of all life led as though by some devilish Fall to the hunting and herding of man by man."[2]

Reading that, I had to wonder if sport, which mimics the language and emotional intensity of war but eliminates the fatal destruction, may be a form of redemption. It not only sublimates that ancient hunting instinct but transforms it into something that can arouse and motivate modern humans as almost nothing else can. The ancient Olympics may have been the first large-scale effort of civilized humanity—whether or not it was the conscious intention at the time—to redirect the war-making impulse to an activity that enabled young men and women to be heroes without having to die. And maybe that, too, was a part of what captivated JFK. In his "Soft American" article, he had alluded almost wistfully to the nobility of that historic experiment. He would not live to see the ugly setbacks that would come with the murders of Israeli athletes at the 1972 Olympics, or the jingoist exploitation of Olympic audiences by the broadcast media, or the huge commercialization that would follow (not to mention the US Olympic Committee's running-shoe endorsement scandal, which made a travesty of Olympic idealism). Redemption is one of those faltering, two-steps-forward, one-step-back transformations that seem frustratingly slow within the blink-of-an-eye moment of our time, but may also be one of our saving graces. The World Cup of soccer, World Series, Super Bowl, NBA championship, Tour de France, Chicago and New York Marathons—and, yes, the Olympics, despite its missteps—along with thousands of less-publicized contests like the one I was engaged in now, together ignite the passions of far more of the world's population than have any wars since the end of World War II. Many more wars had happened since then, but virtually all were tinged by an aura of hard necessity and regret.

The world was a very different place in 1861; that year, a crowd of ebullient spectators had traveled out from Washington to watch the Battle of Bull Run (not far from Manassas, where I now lived), and a magazine illustration of that outing was captioned, "Watching the Federal army advance seemed like a perfect Sunday afternoon diversion." A *London Times* correspondent who joined the crowd wrote, "The spectators were all excited, and a lady with an opera glass who was near me was quite beside herself when an unusually heavy discharge roused the current of her blood—'That is splendid, Oh my! Is not that first rate?'"[3] Such a response by civilians to the mass killing of humans, even if the killing was deemed unavoidable, seemed unimaginable now. Since the high-speed obliterations of Hiroshima and Nagasaki, there had been some kind of global transformation in the collective empathy of our species. The crowd I would soon encounter at Antietam would be of the same species (and even some of the same bloodlines) as the spectators at Bull Run, yet it had been fundamentally transformed. Biologically, we hadn't changed appreciably in a hundred thousand years. But culturally, since Bull Run and Antietam, we'd been changed forever—by two global scorched-earth wars and, arising from them, stupendous leaps in our abilities both to build weapons of quick mass destruction and to more consciously grasp the consequences of such destruction for our humanity.

At least two of the transformative figures I encountered in my work had turned away from the quick-solution sprint economy to take a path of quiet redemption that—again, to quote Robert Frost—could make "all the difference." The first was Ted Taylor. The second was Mikhail Gorbachev, last president of the Soviet Union before its astonishing dismantling in 1991. When I first met Gorbachev at a dinner in New York in 2000, I was transfixed by the potentially apocalyptic connection that had once prevailed between him and Taylor—and that had been defused in a real-life, global enactment of one of those movie scenes in which a bomb is defused just as the timing device ticks down: 3 . . . 2 . . . 1 . . .

I knew about the connection between Taylor and Gorbachev in an abstract way, but it had become vividly personalized one day a few years ago when I came across a journal note Taylor had written about an experience he had at the height of the Cold War:

> A 45-year-old memory haunts me still. It was November 15, 1950. And I had been working at Los Alamos on a much more powerful fission weapon than people had previously thought possible, the Super Oralloy Bomb, or S.O.B.
>
> But now I was at a bar in a Washington hotel, feeling sad and angry because our second daughter, Kathy, was being born that night in Los Alamos. Instead of being with my wife, Caro, I had spent the day at a military intelligence office, poring over aerial photographs of Moscow, placing the sharp point of a compass in Red Square and drawing circles corresponding to the distances at which moderate and severe damage would result from the explosion of different heights of a 500-kiloton made-in-America bomb.[4]

Recalling that note, I had to wonder: How could such a contemplative and caring man once have been so coolly calculating in his work? Five hundred kilotons was enough to incinerate thirty-seven cities the size of Hiroshima, and it would have done an apocalyptic job on Moscow. It was not that Ted had become a different person by the time I met him; I felt certain of that. People don't easily change their basic nature, even when they do have a great change of heart. While we probably can't do much to change what we are, how we *use* what we are can make all the difference. What affected me most about Ted Taylor was not his warnings and scenarios, but his complete reversal of direction. His meditive nature reminded me of the Quaker elders I grew up hearing at Sunday meetings in Plainfield and Summit, New Jersey. Those thoughtful women and men never seemed bitter or angry, even though some of the topics they stood up to address could be infuriating to others. One elder would rise and speak, then sit down. There might be five or ten minutes of silence, then another would stand and add a reflection, or perhaps a quiet counterpoint. At the IR&T office, as Ted walked back and forth, with his hand in his pocket jingling his coins, a lot of his thought involved dreaming about the human future—not a future of conflicting worldviews and war, but of ingenious human interplay with the environment that produced us.

That, too, had profoundly affected my experience of running. A "Cold War" attitude toward sport might have been to regard my opponents as enemies to defeat, rather than as companions in a great adventure. It took me a long time to learn, but I knew now that the more I could let go of the adversarial reflex, the more energy I'd have for running. Conflict poisons the spirit, and probably the blood. Companionship strengthens the spirit. If I wanted to run my best in this race, I needed to remind myself that Frank Probst and all my rivals in the over-sixty division, and all the Marines and army and navy guys, and everyone else who'd taken off from Boonsboro this morning, were among the best companions for a day—or a lifetime—I could ever hope to have. It might be a paradox that would only irritate an old-school coach, but I knew well that I would run my best by hoping that everyone else ran *their* best.

When I met Gorbachev and shook his hand, I felt the same tactile surprise I experienced when I met Muhammad Ali—this was not the iron fist that had once ruled the world. These were gentle handshakes of men who'd grown older but stronger. The dinner had been put on by Green Cross

International, the environmental group Gorbachev set up to help redirect global priorities from the madness of MAD (Mutual Assured Destruction by nuclear holocaust, as depicted in the movie *Doctor Strangelove*) to a restoration of the planet we'd been abusing. What transfixed me was the realization that this was the man who'd been at the very center of Taylor's crosshairs that December night in Washington.

■ ■ ■

I was passing mile post 69, which would mean I was at about the marathon mark, although there was nothing there to indicate so. At twenty-six miles, an ultrarunner can't afford to feel the way he or she would feel at the end of a marathon, since there's still almost another marathon to go. I focused on the fact that I was just a mile from Antietam, which is a kind of psychological landmark: You are now well past the midpoint of the race. I dared to wonder whether the friendly crowd I'd meet there—with not a hint of the bitter divisiveness of their ancestors—would be not just another manifestation of the denial that had crippled our country, but a sign of the healing I could still hope for. Maybe people who could forego a Saturday morning of watching TV sitcoms to go out and cheer for their kids or spouses or friends who were running fifty miles for no discernible purpose or profit or fame were—whether or not they thought of it this way—enjoying something that really was redemptive.

The wind continued pushing, and again I felt that tension—that "cognitive dissonance," as my psych professor at Swarthmore had called it—stemming not only from the companionable closeness of bitter legacies with friendly spectators, and war with sport, but also of frantic speed with stillness. And it was not just that the monuments of a long-ago war now flanked this course in silent stillness; the whole countryside around here was like that. For all the horrific and world-shaking events that had occurred here, it was now pastoral and peaceful wherever I looked. I knew enough about ecology to recognize that this was by no means wilderness, and was in many ways disturbed and destabilized. The towpath and canal were artificial structures, sections of which had been destroyed by hurricanes several times and would someday be destroyed again—perhaps to an extent that they could not be rebuilt. But the river and woods had adapted in their own ways; stately beech and rust-hued maple trees flanked the towpath, and a couple of months ago on a segment of the canal that still contained water, just upstream from Georgetown, I'd seen painted turtles sunning themselves on a half-submerged log. It was a peaceable kingdom I was running through; this whole region was.

Two days ago, driving from our home in Manassas up to the JFK headquarters hotel in Hagerstown, I had decided not to take the quickest route, Interstate 270, but to follow a more pastoral route through Loudoun County, Virginia—through the little town of Hillsboro (with a population of one hundred), where every structure dated from the late 1800s or earlier, then out through the rolling Virginia wine country, across the Potomac at a point that put us in Maryland just a mile from Weverton, and up Rohrersville Road along the valley parallel to the South Mountain ridge on our right, to Boonsboro. We drove past fields and scattered farmhouses and small graveyards and splashes of late-fall orange and yellow foliage, all of which made me think of a Grandma Moses painting. And then we traveled from Boonsboro to Hagerstown, where a thousand runners were gathering.

On the drive we passed very few other cars. Once we left the outer Washington suburb of Leesburg, we saw hardly any people at all—even when passing through the old towns of Hillsboro and Boonsboro. A faint scent of apple cider hung in the air, and it took me back to my college days forty years ago, when a group of us cross-country runners would take a Sunday run, bare-chested, through the quiet countryside of the Quaker state. Throughout the trip, the prevailing feel was of stillness. It calmed my troubled soul and both steadied me and psyched me for the run. When the running is good, there's nothing like it.

8

KILLIANSBURG CAVE

Becoming a Persistence Hunter: The
Long Day of Tracking, the Grateful
Kill, the Celebration

HEADING NORTH FROM Antietam, the towpath seemed to get
wilder—the trees larger and more gnarled, the canal to my
right more tangled with overgrowth. The last sounds of the
spectators faded, and, after a period of silence that could
have been either five minutes or the hundred years it takes
for a Quaker kid to sit through Sunday meeting, I found myself glancing left and right, the way I'd been taught as a teenager to drive a car—keep your eyes moving, don't get fixated
on the road straight ahead. Maybe that was a vestige of the
hunter-gatherer's need to read his surroundings. Paul
Shepard noted that many indigenous peoples can identify as
many as two thousand plants in the wild, and that there's a
tribe in Colombia whose members can distinguish between
two hundred different species of a single genus by sight and
name—and by their respective medical, nutritive, ecological,
and utilitarian uses. Those of us who live in the consumer

culture? We can identify hundreds of brand-name products made from the exhumed remains of plants that died four hundred million years ago and have been recently turned into plastic.

After a while, across the canal to my right, I began to see cliffs where hikers had discovered a number of caves. Accounts of that "bloodiest day" at Antietam record that the battle continued sporadically for another two days, and during that time some of the residents of nearby Sharpsburg took refuge in what is now called Killiansburg Cave. They remained hidden there until Robert E. Lee and his decimated Virginia militia retreated over a shallow Potomac crossing called Pack Horse Ford. The ford would be somewhere downstream from here, down the heavily wooded embankment to my left.

Retreat to caves and canyons, whether to escape ice-age storms, predators, or other humans, has been a survival strategy for humans for millennia, at least since the last glacial maximum thirteen thousand years ago, and possibly since our long-distance-walking *Homo erectus* predecessors roamed the planet a million and a half years before that—and has continued to be used right up to our own time. The Tarahumara escaped the guns and swords of the Spanish Conquistadors by disappearing into the vast Copper Canyon four centuries ago, relying on their long-distance running mobility much as their South American brethren, the Incas, did. The Incas deployed their long-distance relay-running couriers, the Chasquis, to carry messages over the rugged roads of the Andes faster than the Spanish could communicate around the coasts by ship. Centuries later, in the American West, the Apache rebel Geronimo and thirty-eight of his warriors, the last holdouts of the Indian Wars, evaded the hot pursuit of eight thousand US and Mexican Army soldiers and a thousand armed vigilantes by disappearing into the Arizona mountain canyons without a single one of them being caught. And historically, both the good guys and the bad had used canyons and caves this way. Even now, as I ran, Osama bin Laden was apparently hiding somewhere in the caves of Tora Bora, in Afghanistan. As of the 6 o'clock news last night, which I watched before turning in early, I hadn't heard any news of his having been caught.

Of course, we now knew that the caves of the prehistoric "cavemen" were not only refuges but, for some, places for home and hearth and evidently even a vivid form of storytelling. Recent research has established that the stereotypical image of cavemen I'd grown up with was mistaken. Maybe that image of hulking, slope-headed, hairy brutes with clubs could be traced to the seventeenth-century philosopher Thomas Hobbes, who famously wrote that the life of a human living in a state of nature, before civilization, was "solitary, poor, nasty, brutish, and short."[1] Or, as further condensed in more recent, more hurried times, just "nasty, brutish, and short."

Hobbes's comment underpinned what was to become an almost never-questioned premise of human history: that the advent of agriculture, with its abundance of farm fruits, grains, and livestock, had liberated humans from having to hunt and gather to survive, and had been the launch of the civilization we now enjoy. Lester R. Brown had been one of the first students of agricultural science to question that view, in his research at the US Department of Agriculture, and then in his groundbreaking book, *The Twenty-Ninth Day*. When I first went to work for Brown at Worldwatch, I was overwhelmed by the emerging evidence the institute's researchers were gathering, that the pleasures of the foods we now enjoyed had come at staggering costs. The view of the mainstream historians was that agriculture—the transformation of

KILLIANSBURG CAVE

wild plants and animals into domesticated crops and herds—had been the greatest chapter of the human story.

The historian Jared Diamond, however, would offer a radically different assessment. In an article he titled "The Worst Mistake in the History of the Human Race," he wrote: "Recent discoveries suggest that the adoption of agriculture, supposedly our most decisive step to a better life, was in many ways a catastrophe from which we have never recovered."[2] The standard view of history was that we modern humans obviously live far better than the miserable serfs of the medieval times did, and that medieval people of course had lived better than the cavemen had. That view was called *progressivist* because it assumed that human history is always a story of continued progress. A big part of it, I knew, was the assumption of mainstream economists that a "strong" economy must be a *perpetually growing* economy, quite regardless of the fact that we have become an exploding population on a planet of finite size and limited resources.

In his challenge to that view, Diamond cited newly discovered evidence that the life of prehistoric humans had apparently not been at all what Thomas Hobbes and the progressivists thought. The evidence included both forensic studies of ancient human remains and anthropological studies of the few hunter-gatherer societies that still thrived today. Particularly notable were the findings of paleopathologists that the average height of hunter-gatherers toward the end of the ice ages was five feet, nine inches for men and five feet, five inches for women—about the same as they were for men and women at the start of the twenty-first century.

Of course, those were also the approximate average heights of the very healthy and fit men and women in this JFK race. Contrary to traditional belief, prehistoric humans had evidently not been stunted by dietary deficiency.

The contemporary evidence confirmed it. Researchers, to the surprise of almost everyone, had found that so-called primitive peoples, such as the Tarahumara in Copper Canyon, the Kalahari Bushmen of southern Africa, and the Hadza nomads of the Rift Valley in Tanzania, were not worse off than farmers in either their access to food or their hours spent working. Contrary to our long-held assumptions, these modern hunter-gatherers spent only twelve to nineteen hours per week to obtain enough food from the wild to live well, including whatever time was needed to chase down wildebeest or deer. Interestingly, the number of hours they spent hunting and gathering was about the same as the number it takes to train for a marathon or ultra. A significant result: the contemporary hunter-gatherers had *more* time than we of the sprint economy do to relax, spend time with their families, engage in recreational or artistic pursuits, and maybe even reflect on the meaning of their life on this planet. The downside is that they didn't have fighter jets.

In a way, I was even a bit envious. Wouldn't it be great if, after this race, I didn't have to go right back to my office on Monday?

Hobbes, of course, lived too soon to appreciate those hunter-gatherer studies—as did, for that matter, the teachers who instructed my generation in school. So, our view may have been badly distorted by what our teachers *did* know— that *farmers in medieval times* lived a life that was, unquestionably, nasty, brutish, and short. But at least they'd had hovels. It was easy to assume that if prehistoric people had to live in caves instead of at least having thatch-roofed huts to call home, and had to go search for something to eat in a wilderness full of dangers instead of at least being able to grab a scrawny chicken from the yard, life for them must have been even worse. In recent decades, however, anthropologists confirmed that most humans never lived in caves to begin with, and that those who did tell a very different story.

What the Hobbesians could not have known was that the life of a Paleolithic persistence runner-gatherer was evidently far less deprived and unhealthy than that of a medieval serf. "It's almost inconceivable that Bushmen, who eat 75 or so wild plants, could die of starvation the way hundreds of thousands of Irish farmers and their families did during the potato famine of the 1840s," wrote Jared Diamond.[3] By medieval times, and continuing into the time of the Irish famine and then *our* time, the domestication of plants and animals had greatly simplified human food sources and drastically reduced the genetic diversity and nutrient content that nurtures health and immunity to disease. And as a result, the average heights of humans had been severely *stunted* with the rise of civilization. Skeletal remains confirmed that by the Middle Ages, average heights had drastically *shrunk* from Paleolithic times, by half a foot—to five feet, three inches for men and five feet for women. Civilization had enabled people to mass-produce food for the fast-growing population, but the reliance on agriculture to produce it had separated most people from their wild environs, and the farmed food was now far less nutritious than the wild food had been. It was the first step toward what we in the twenty-first century would call "empty-calorie" food—the kind of monoculture product that would later, as people also became less physically active, cause rates of obesity, diabetes, and heart disease to soar. Civilization had taken a face-plant, at least in Europe. That "worst mistake in human history," said Diamond, had been "thinking human history over the past million years has been a long tale of progress."[4] Some kinds of progress have allowed for a gradual recovery of normal physical height in recent centuries, but continuing erosions of biological diversity—

and our consequent vulnerabilities to degenerative disease and ecological collapse—have only worsened.

Glancing at the cliffs across the canal, I couldn't see the cave opening. I'd found photos taken by hikers and spelunkers, and I knew that while some of the openings would be on the cliff side, visible from the towpath, others—including Killiansburg—were apparently farther up over the rim, hidden by woods. I thought of that more famous cave, called Lascaux, which was also well hidden when first discovered by twentieth-century farmers in France, but when explored revealed astonishing evidence of what may have been the very rich life of prehistoric people—not rich in the powers and products of technology, but in spirit, wonder, and appreciation of the world in which they hunted and gathered.

The paintings on the walls and ceilings of Lascaux are mainly of large animals—the very animals that persistence hunters would have pursued and killed. There are horses, deer, wild cattle, wild cats, and a lone black bear. The rooms and ceilings on which they'd been painted had been given evocative names by their discoverers: the Hall of the Bulls, Chamber of the Feline, Panel of the Chinese Horses, Ceiling of the Red Cows, and Frieze of the Small Stags.

Beyond the artistic exuberance of the paintings (one room had been called the "Sistine Chapel of Prehistory"), two things particularly struck me about this cave. One was that the animals depicted were not particularly indigenous to France as we now know it, but seemed to evoke far-flung parts of the world. Either the people who made those paintings had traveled prodigious distances by foot, or climate change and, later, the coming of civilization, had wiped out much of the wildlife that once thrived in this region. Or, most likely, the people who lived then had traveled from afar *and* the wildlife of the region had since been largely decimated.

The other thing that impressed me about Lascaux was that humans were not the featured attraction. The artists' main interest—the object of what had obviously been great awe and reverence—was the big game. That was a telling phrase, I thought: the *big game*, which is not just about large animals, but about the nature of our species' life on earth. Millennia later, when civilization arose, artistic expression would become brazenly human-centered, and Michelangelo's Sistine Chapel would depict our Creator in human form—and humans as the favored beneficiaries of that creation. Maybe it was inevitable, after the building of walled cities and systemic separation of people from the wild world that had long been our home, that we would begin to *forget*—to unlearn—how dependent we are, for every bite and breath we take, on the thousands of other life forms that are now struggling to survive in the places we have not yet plowed or bulldozed.

In twentieth-century America, maybe in an instinctive as well as educated reaction to the Industrial Revolution and its escalating effects, a wide range of radical thinkers began identifying human-centered views of the world as having become, ironically, the greatest threat to the human future. "A focus on anthropomorphism as a major root cause of the ecological crisis had been made by Thoreau, Muir, and more recent writers such as Robinson Jeffers, D. H. Lawrence, Aldo Leopold, Aldous Huxley, and Loren Eisley," the philosopher George Sessions recently noted.[5] Their work launched the modern environmental movement, a guiding premise of which was that we humans cannot dominate the earth for long, and that we will need to rediscover its nature—and our own—or risk losing it.

Modern runners, perhaps especially in our migration from the roads to the trails over the past twenty years, were perhaps beginning to do some of that relearning, even if we didn't think of it in those terms. As Paul Shepard wrote, "Men are born human. What they must learn is to be an animal. If they learn otherwise it may kill them and life on the planet. It is very difficult to learn to be an animal. First man must unlearn his conception of an animal as a brute."[6]

The paintings at Lascaux seemed to leave signs of a society in which neither the animals nor the humans were seen as brutes in the sense Hobbes meant. Among the scores of paintings, none depicted a hunter triumphantly bringing down his prey or lording it over a fallen beast. None offered the Paleolithic equivalent of a moose head on a hunting-lodge wall. The animals commemorated by those paintings were not trophies, but beautifully alive, and I felt sure they had not just been lugged home and devoured, but revered and thanked for giving their lives so that the hunters and their families might live. There had been no psychological separation between the acts of killing an animal, appreciating it, and eating it.

By the time of industrial agriculture, the separation brought by domestication—not only of plants and animals, but of us, the humans who'd accomplished it—was more or less complete. To a twentieth or twenty-first-century American, a hamburger is not the remains of a steer. The animal isn't what you think of when you stand in line at Burger King. Bacon is not a pig, and "wings" are not pieces cut off of a bird. Our disconnection from the sources of our food is part of a larger disconnection that now endangers our whole future. The poet-farmer Wendell Berry, in his 1977 book *The Unsettling of America,* wrote:

> The modern urban-industrial society is based
> on a series of radical disconnections between
> body and soul, husband and wife, marriage and

community, community and earth. At each of these points of disconnection, the collaboration of corporation, government, and experts sets up a profit-making enterprise that results in the further dismemberment and impoverishment of the Creation.[7]

Up ahead I spotted mile post 73 and struggled to do the calculation: Post 70 had been about mile twenty-eight of the JFK course, just past Antietam, so this should be about thirty-one miles into the race. Oddly, although running always stimulated my imagination, it somehow made even the simplest arithmetic more difficult. Left brain/right brain? I have no idea.

As I lifted my arm to check my watch, a young Marine pulled even on the left, matching strides with me. He glanced at my elbow and leg, and said, "You're bleeding, sir." I laughed, and then I thought, *Good God, I'm not just losing water through my pores, but through my knee!* I was also a little too woozy (why the stupid laugh?) and knew I must be getting dehydrated. I'd need to do some serious drinking at Snyder's Landing.

At the same time, I was feeling another lift. For one thing, thirty-one miles is fifty kilometers, so I was now moving into true ultra territory. For another, evidently not all of the Marines had been ahead of me after all. And right now it was *high noon*, time for a showdown! My better angels cautioned me, though—I'd need to be patient for another couple of hours at least. And I didn't carry a gun, like all the cowboys in *High Noon* did; I just carried a water bottle. The only animals I'd ever killed were a copperhead I almost stepped on once, about two feet from the door of my cabin, a rattlesnake that got too close to Elizabeth when she was six, and one groundhog. The snakes I had killed with a shovel, with great reluctance, and the groundhog with a rock, in a sort of accident.

I felt bad about the groundhog. It was the summer of my nineteenth year, and I was out for a long run in the Green Mountains of Vermont on a trail I'd never been on before. It would soon be dark, and I wondered if I might be lost—and felt a trickle of adrenaline in my gut. Just then, crossing the trail about ninety feet ahead of me, I saw a groundhog. Without thinking, I picked up a stone about the size of a baseball and threw it at the animal, of course assuming I'd miss. I'd been a pitcher in Little League one summer and hadn't been very good at finding the strike zone. To my great surprise, the stone hit the groundhog on the head and it fell over, dead. It was as if running had put my whole body, including my shoulder and arm, more in synch. Also without thinking, I picked up the animal and carried it back to the camp where I was staying. The next morning I skinned it, imagining that I was an Indian and was obligated to make something useful out of the pelt. But no one had ever taught me how to cure a pelt, and after a few days I had to bury it.

Now, four decades later, I often wondered what it was like to be a persistence hunter—which, genetically, I still was. The University of Utah researcher David Carrier had provoked the curiosity of his mentor, Dennis Bramble, about that with his landmark "Energetic Paradox" article in 1984, observing that humans actually ran with lower energy efficiency than the animals they chased—yet prevailed in pursuits over long distances. How could that be? In subsequent years, Bramble and his colleague Daniel Lieberman, a professor of human evolutionary biology at Harvard, undertook a series of investigations to determine what anatomical and physiological features distinguish a vertebrate that primarily runs from one that primarily walks. Several million years ago, the earlier hominids had been walkers.

Bramble and Lieberman identified twenty-six specific characteristics that separated the runners from the walkers, and found—much to the surprise and fascination of scientists everywhere—that in every one of the twenty-six categories, modern humans belong to the running group. At least one of those features, bare skin, was *uniquely* human. And as the investigation progressed, it became clear that in humans particularly, some of the other features that enhanced our running abilities—including the shape of our heads and structure of our necks—were intimately related to the function of our bare skin.

I didn't know it at the time of the 2001 JFK race, but Bramble and Lieberman were on their way to a momentous breakthrough in our understanding of human evolution—and indeed of human nature itself. The anatomical studies were compelling, but evolutionary science had long been wedded to the idea that humans evolved as walkers, not runners. The famous discovery of the early hominid "Lucy" had fascinated the scientific world with the revelation that this most ancient of women had walked on two legs. And she was anatomically adapted to walking, not running. The new anatomical findings needed to be reconciled with the hominid fossil record, and the breakthrough would come with an observation that—once it was articulated—gave the scientists an almost epiphanic clarification. Lucy had been a member of an earlier species of hominid, *Australopithecus afarensis*, which walked the earth for over two million years, long before *Homo sapiens* emerged. Lucy's species had a considerably smaller brain than modern humans have and even over its million years did not begin to show the rapid development of modern humans' ability to envision, anticipate, and persist—an ability that arguably originated with the complex endeavor of the persistence hunt.

"The feature that differentiates hominids from other primates is not large brain size, but the set of characteristics associated with erect bipedal posture and a striding gait," David Carrier wrote.[8] The epiphany was that the development of modern humans' bigger brain and the evolving strategy not only for surviving but for becoming conscious explorers, adapters, and manipulators of our environment coincided with the appearance of traits that enabled a transition from bipedal walking to long-distance bipedal running, and especially to running in a hot climate.

"There were 2.5 to 3 million years of bipedal walking [by *Australopithecines*] without even looking like a human," Bramble would write. "So is walking going to be what suddenly transforms the hominid body? . . . No, walking won't do that, but running will."[9] Adaptation to endurance running, for example, altered the human torso to allow the shoulders to turn independently of the head, which allowed the head to remain fairly still even as the arms swing, thereby enhancing stability and balance—an important development for an animal running on two legs instead of four. Joan Benoit recalled in her 1987 book *Running Tide* that on the day of the very first race she ever ran, in a track meet at the age of eight, she watched an earlier event that made a lasting impression on her. It was an 880-yard run (half-mile) for teenage boys, and she was fascinated. "I was trying to figure out what made the lead runner look so good," she wrote. And then she saw the answer: "His head . . . hardly moved—he used his energy to power his legs."[10] But, of course, even though his head hardly moved, his arms were swinging. She took that observation to heart and won her own race. And nineteen years later, she would win the gold medal in the first-ever Olympic marathon for women.

■ ■ ■

Reflecting on the epic journey our species had taken since

that prehistoric transition from the relatively unchanging life
of *Australopithecines* to the running and then racing and then
all-out sprinting life of *Homo sapiens*, I thought of the mission
statement that Ted Taylor and my brother Bob had written
three decades ago about the conundrum of ever-expanding
human capability: "Technology, for all its impact on the
world, cannot be 'good' or 'bad.' It can save lives and it can
kill; it can intensify the pleasures of life or it can fill the world
with misery." It's what we *do* with the technology, including
agricultural technology, that makes all the difference. And it
struck me that that's equally true of what we do with our bodies, which were the original models for—and controllers of—
our technologies. Over the past century, in the thrall of the
Industrial and Post-Industrial revolutions, we had increasingly marginalized and even abandoned our bodies.

President Kennedy had seen it, even if his picture of what
had happened was still incomplete. Possibly the most egre-
gious aspect of the abandonment had been the spreading
belief that the good life is a life of ever-increasing convenience and ease, in which hard work is no longer necessary.
But hard work (as distinguished from brutish work!) was
what brought the early human hunter to the feast and to the
celebration of his good fortune, and it was what inspired his
art. And we were his direct descendants; we had the same
genes and anatomy, the same deep drive to envision and pursue and persist—and work hard, as long as we could breathe.
And, of course, we had the same bare skin to cool the heat of
our extraordinary metabolism.

I thought of that familiar phrase, "No sweat!" which so
aptly expressed how duped we'd been by the lure of an effort-

less, technology-augmented existence, and it seemed to me that that expression could be an epitaph for a species that loses its way. End war? No sweat! Lose weight? No sweat!

Despite the wind off the Potomac, I could feel the sweat running down my face and neck. I really needed that refill, and, thank God, Snyder's Landing was just minutes away. I eased up a little and was immediately passed by a navy kid and a slim young woman running side by side. I felt a bit of older-man's envy, but also felt my spirits lift. Both he and she, like the Marine who'd passed a few minutes ago, looked quite liberated from the imprisoning stereotypes I'd grown up with: the hardened warrior with his heavy equipment, boots, and armor; the vulnerable female with her nylons and girdle and falsies and heels who couldn't possibly do something like run a long distance. Even as recently as the early 1980s, the Olympics had not allowed women to compete in races that would last longer than about five minutes. These two looked light on their feet, relaxed, conversing amiably—just a couple of young people enjoying the day, in a world that might have a future yet.

9

SNYDER'S LANDING

The Energy-Supply Illusion: Carbo-
Loading, Body Heat, and Naked Skin

AT A LOT of the aid stations I see in an ultra, I don't stop. Or
I pause just long enough to swallow a paper cupful of water
and refill my hand-bottle with electrolyte drink—and then
hurry back to the trail. I don't want to rush but also don't
want to waste any time. At Snyder's, though, I needed to stop.
Support crews had difficulty getting to the aid stations along
the towpath via narrow, unmarked rural roads on which it
was easy to get lost, and I had asked Sharon not to try. I would
cope.

Generally, the aid station tables in an ultra, laden with
stuff to eat, don't appeal to me. In their promotional literature and Web sites, ultras often feature well-stocked aid stations as particular attractions: big spreads of bananas, candy,
peanut butter and jelly sandwiches, oranges, Gatorade, potato chips, watermelon, pretzels, Advil, PowerBars, Clif Bars,
soup, and, most ubiquitously, electrolyte drink of unknown

provenance—the runner's equivalent of that old summer-camp standby, "mystery meat."

These tables always made me slightly queasy. Right now, there was only one thing I felt like eating—a boiled potato. I found one, much to my relief, took a bite with the efficiency of a NASCAR driver getting a tire change, and got back into the race.

Last evening, for my pre-race meal, I'd had a sandwich. Many of the runners had gone to the big carbo-loading dinner in the hotel's banquet room, but Sharon and I, and Elizabeth, had decided to stay in our room so I could eat and go to bed early. I'm not a backyard-grill kind of guy, but I'm good with a loaf of whole grain bread. I made us sandwiches of aged cheddar cheese, organic lettuce and tomato, avocado, mustard and mayo, and fruit. To drink, we had unfiltered apple juice and spring water.

When I was a kid in the 1940s and early '50s, a sandwich like that would have been hard to find or even make. There were very few "health food" stores, as we called them in those days. The ones you could find sold mainly things like powdered kelp or bottles of cod liver oil or jars of brewer's yeast. The bread they sold was heavy and dark—I think it was imported from the Black Forest, and a loaf of it was so dense it could have been used for firewood. My mother gave me sandwiches for my school lunch made with what she called "brown bread," which she baked herself—not as dense as the health-food bread, but still not *normal*—and I was so embarrassed that I usually threw the sandwich in the schoolyard trash can rather than be seen with it. All the other kids had Wonder Bread!

I had never dreamed, as an elementary and junior high school kid, that I would soon discover fresh-baked, organic whole grain breads that tasted way better than the cottonlike, bleached white bread I once coveted. (Or that I'd wake up to discover that my mother's bread was really good, if I didn't judge its taste by the "yuck!" reactions of other kids!) I never dreamed that by the year 2001 there would be a fast-growing chain of brightly lit, natural-foods supermarkets in most US cities, where you could find beautiful fresh fruits and vegetables that had not been sprayed with pesticides . . . and freshly baked whole grain breads that had no chemical preservatives, and peanut butter that was not processed with hydrogenated fat. The phenomenon of the urban natural-foods co-ops of the 1970s, with their tie-dye T-shirted managers and customers, to say nothing of the Whole Foods Markets and organic-foods sections of supermarkets that would follow a couple of decades later, were not yet on the horizon when I was a kid. But in 1955, my understanding of food underwent a radical transformation.

My father, a very quiet and stoic man who rarely complained about anything, had been brushed off when he occasionally asked his long-time employers at AT&T if he could be moved to an office where he didn't have to breathe the secondhand smoke of the other men (all of whom were chain-smokers in an era when a man who didn't smoke might have his masculinity questioned). He finally succumbed to his chronic asthma and had to take a leave of absence. Somehow, he got connected with a radical doctor, a man who was regarded by the American Medical Association about the same way a woman believed to be a witch was regarded by the Puritan fathers.

The doctor was blunt. If my father wanted to live much longer, he needed to do three things: Eliminate all highly refined foods from his diet, eliminate hydrogenated fats, and eliminate chemical additives. I don't recall the name of the doctor, but today I am still amazed at how prescient he turned out to be—and how fortunate (or astute at doctor-choosing) was my father, who followed that radical advice and recov-

ered well enough to live another thirty-five years and continue working at AT&T for another fifteen, without ever
getting sick again. (When he died, at age eighty-nine, it
wasn't in a hospital bed, but in his favorite reading chair; according to my mother, he simply put his head back one afternoon and closed his eyes and was gone.)

As it happened, I decided to adopt that diet too. It was
very close to what would later be called a "Paleo" diet. The
year was 1954, and Roger Bannister had just set the sporting
world agog by running the first four-minute mile. It was also,
for me, that pivotal adolescent time when a kid's interests
begin to change. I was thirteen and had discovered that I
liked to run, and Bannister's achievement captivated me. Although I hadn't had any problem with asthma myself, I'd had
a few bouts of bronchitis. And more significantly, as I listened
to the maverick doctor talking to my father, something about
what he said sounded right. The way Americans ate in the
1950s was an unfortunate change from the way people had
eaten for thousands of years, he said. All that Coca-Cola,
Wonder Bread, and Crisco was not *natural.* This was long before the word *natural* became part of the currency of food
marketing and advertising, and the logic of it seemed to me
unarguable. If refined sugars and grains could mess up your
blood sugar and send you crashing in just hours, as the doctor said, what might they do over months and years? My interest in both avoiding my father's debilitation and maximizing
my potential as a runner galvanized my determination to follow a strict natural-foods diet from then on.

Somehow I got it into my head that if this diet was good for
helping a sick person get well, it might also be good for helping a well person get even *more well*—or for helping a strong
runner get stronger. It was, you might say, my first introduction
to the concept of "quality of life," and without any prompting

I joined my father in adopting the new diet. By the morning of the 2001 JFK 50 Mile, I hadn't consumed white sugar, white bread, or hydrogenated fat in forty-six years. And I hadn't had a soft drink in my life, since my mother with her brown bread and organic gardening thing had never approved of sodas, and I had just never gotten started. And by 2001, I'd gone about thirty years without meat as well. Maybe the hunter in me, having figured out that I no longer live in a world of vast wilderness, had learned to sublimate the kill. My spear-thrust now would be my final kick to the finish.

When I went to a natural-foods co-op in the 1970s, I loved the spirit of the kids—it *was* mostly kids—who were both the managers and customers. The one I went to most often, in Washington, DC, was called *Yes!* Cities like New York, San Francisco, Boston, Philadelphia, Austin, Seattle, and Portland all had one or more of these places, and the proprietors were usually people who made conscious connections between what they were selling and how they wanted to live. I thought it was no coincidence that the managers of the dominant supermarket chains didn't seem to make such connections at all—not even now, four decades later. Sometimes I'd walk into one of these chain supermarkets and find myself wondering how it can be that those managers can blithely sell cigarettes just a few feet from the fresh vegetables, or products loaded with hydrogenated or "trans" fats right next to products advertising their "fat free" ingredients. An in-store pharmacy will dispense obscenely expensive weight-reduction and heart-care drugs a few feet away from displays of candy, soft drinks, and hundreds of obesity-inducing and arterial plaque-building products. Don't the executives of these companies see the disconnect? Do they really believe it's just a matter of "personal choice" whether you get healthy or accidently kill yourself? As Wendell Berry said, the disconnection was omnipresent.

But that, in fact, was the essence of the problem our sprint culture brought us. We had created an economy *based* on thoughtless disconnection. That way, the supermarket manager, who was probably a nice guy, didn't have to *think* about the eventual effects of the products he sold—either the effects of how they were produced or of how they'd be consumed. The economy of disconnection, like a classic pyramid scheme, achieved its profits by fragmenting information so that none of the participants see the scheme as a whole. In a Ponzi scheme, new investors don't see that their money is being fraudulently used to pay earlier investors, rather than used to grow their wealth. In the sprint culture, the newest apps-happy American teenagers didn't see that their cell phones, fried chicken, and sports shoes were often being paid for by the lives of other teenagers trapped in sweatshops or caught up in resource wars in Congo or Nigeria or Brazil, and that sooner or later the demons loosed by those wars might come home to roost. What had happened on a regional basis in places like Sudan or Afghanistan or Kosovo, or other internecine conflicts, could continue to metastasize. *Antietam could be back*, shape-shifted as Orwell predicted, vastly larger as Thomas Malthus and Paul Ehrlich and Lester Brown all warned, and with unthinkable consequences as Ted Taylor and my brother Bob and Mikhail Gorbachev all worried.

■ ■ ■

I glanced at my watch and felt another trickle of anxiety. There were a good seventeen miles yet to go, and although I was still on target—barely—to break eight hours, I was pooped. Both my bowels and my stomach were empty. Energy flow is dependent on a continuous process of fuel input and waste output—whether in a single person or a whole civilization. But in both realms, I knew, there was an entrenched misconception—the idea that it's all about *supply*. In American industry and policy, energy input was virtually *defined* as supply. The country's response to the oil crisis of 1973 had been to do whatever was needed to ramp up supply—whether by drilling for more oil in Alaskan wilderness, lopping off more West Virginia mountaintops for coal, or flexing more military muscle in the oil-rich Middle East.

The supply-equals-input equation had understandably shaped beliefs about energy inputs in high-energy sports as well. In 1965, a professor of medicine at the University of Florida, J. Robert Cade, concocted a mixture of sugar and electrolytes he called Gatorade, which in the early 1970s fueled a boom in the athletic energy-supply market. In the 1980s, a distance runner named Brian Maxwell started selling a product he called PowerBars, which he later sold to the Nestle Corporation for $385 million. By the 1990s, energy bars and drinks filled whole shelves in supermarkets.

Among physicists and engineers, however, it wasn't at all that simple. A nonprofit research group, the American Council for an Energy-Efficient Economy (ACEEE), conducted a breakthrough study showing that three-fourths of America's increase in industrial output over a thirty-eight-year span had been provided *not* by increased energy supply but by increased energy *efficiency*. As a long-time runner, I wasn't taken entirely by surprise. While the performances of elite runners had improved over the years, they hadn't improved nearly as much as the consumption of athletic energy drinks and supplements had. When I'd won this race in 6 hours, 4 minutes in 1977, there had been very little in the way of aid stations, and I had consumed only a modicum of homemade energy drink handed to me by Sharon. Yet, last year, in this era of abundant energy supplements, only one of the 703 finishers had run faster on this course than I did twenty-three years earlier.

The now-too-neglected secret, I knew, was that the body's output, like industry's, was more strongly determined by energy efficiency than by supply. Both were needed, but efficiency was by far the bigger factor. Elite runners had to know this, at least subconsciously. Dedicated training has the effect of *increasing the distance a particular individual can run per hundred calories consumed.* If an untrained man tried to run a marathon simply by relying on supply and consuming an energy bar every half-mile, he'd still probably have to be picked up by the meat wagon before he got halfway through the race. If a friend of his who had trained for months went the whole distance and did well, it would be because he was relying far more on the efficiency with which he used the energy he already had in him when the race started, than on anything he consumed along the way.

The efficiency secret was little recognized in industry partly because the fossil-fuel companies had a huge vested interest in supply. Greater energy efficiency could reduce demand, which would be bad for fuel sales. But a more hidden reason is that most people seem to have only a sketchy understanding of what efficiency really is. Most of us know what it *means,* but not much about the science of how it is actually achieved, whether in an electric hot water heater or in an athlete's body.

A runner I knew, whom I won't name because he might be embarrassed by what happened, had assumed what most people assumed: that energy efficiency is a simple ratio between input and output. He had run fifty-milers successfully a few times and decided to enter the famous Western States 100 Mile in California. In his logistical preparations, he thought he'd burn about 150 calories per mile, so he figured—very mistakenly—that he'd need to take in 15,000 calories. Ergo, he'd need to consume around fifty Power-Bars. As might have been predicted, by the time he got to forty miles and had choked down about twenty of those bars against the protests of a seriously rebelling stomach (the guy wasn't *listening*), he was both very sick and exhausted.

The poor guy's thinking was a perfect reflection of the way Americans have misunderstood energy in the economy at large. A salesman for gas-fired hot water heaters, for example, might tell a customer that his product has 85 percent efficiency because only 15 percent of the heat is lost "up the stack" and therefore 85 percent is going into the water. But a physicist would point out that the gas flame is much, much hotter than the heated water coming out, so a lot of the work that could have been done by that flame has been wasted. In other words, it's the *work* output or loss, not *energy* output or loss, that should be measured. According to the first law of thermodynamics (the law of conservation of energy), energy itself *can't* be used up or lost. What matters is the efficiency with which energy is converted from one form to another, whether in producing hot water, electric power, or the contraction in a runner's legs.

In 1972, a government consultant, Jack Bridges, using the same unscientific logic that the hot-water-heater salesmen used, presented a report to the US Congress asserting that the United States as a whole was using energy with an average efficiency of 50 percent, which he assured the politicians was so high that further gains from efficiency could not be relied on, and that the country would therefore need to build hundreds of new nuclear power plants by the end of the twentieth century. It was the same kind of thinking that led that

Western States newbie to think he'd need lots and lots of PowerBars. But when my physicist brother Bob did his own calculation of US energy efficiency, based on actual engineering principles, later confirmed during his tenure as a professor of engineering and public policy at Carnegie-Mellon University, his US average came to roughly 10 percent. That left room for huge efficiency gains. And as the ACEEE study later confirmed, that was just what occurred over the three decades following the Bridges report—resulting in continued economic growth without *any* new nuclear plants being constructed. And even then, our industries had barely begun to scratch the surface of what they could do to boost output without additional input. Our economy, I thought, could learn a lot from a long-distance runner.

■ ■ ■

I turned my head to look at the sun—a weak winter sun, really. This would be about as warm as it would get today. And that could be a problem. In a long-distance run, you're always juking with balances, no less than a basketball player driving to the hoop through a fast-moving, defensive phalanx of opponents' hips, arms, and hands. For a runner, it may be different balances, but—maybe surprisingly—it's no less complex. As I'd reminded myself over two hours ago, *If you want to make God laugh, tell him you're going to run down the Weverton switchbacks fast without a scratch.* The complexities keep bringing new challenges to those of us who run on two legs.

At this point in the race, my challenge was just the simple motion of turning my head. In my training runs, I'd noticed a curious pattern: After a two- or three-hour run on trails, it was hard to turn my head—my neck was too sore! My routes all started with about a mile on a road before I got to a trailhead, and I had to turn my head to watch for cars when I crossed the road. No problem, of course. But coming back and re-crossing the road, hours later, my neck would be very sore and stiff, even more than my calves or quads—which, in fact, were rarely sore at all. Sometimes, it was actually easier to slow down and jog a little half-circle on the shoulder so I could see down the road without having to turn my head all the way. *Why?*

The answer, I eventually learned, was that the ability to turn the head, independent of the shoulders and torso, is one of those key traits that launched humans on the epic journey that led—for good or ill—to the invention of civilization. I don't mean this metaphorically, although being able to look back in time may indeed be a prerequisite to being able to plan ahead. Here I mean *literally*. It's like the old folk song, "The foot-bone connected to the knee-bone, the knee-bone connected to the thigh-bone, the thigh-bone connected to the hip bone. Oh hear the word of the Lord!" Neck-turn is anatomically connected to the ability to run long distances over rough ground; that ability is cognitively connected to the ability to anticipate what's on the trail ahead; and the ability to anticipate is neurologically connected to the ability to envision, and plan, and invent.

And just what *was* that connection between head turning and civilization inventing? After professors Bramble and Lieberman discovered that the modern human's ability to swing the shoulders and arms while keeping the head fairly still was somewhat critical for enabling an animal on just two legs to maintain physical balance, it struck me that the converse must be true as well. On a rough trail, there might be hundreds of bumps or ruts that threw the body slightly this way or that, while the head and neck instinctively *countered* in order to maintain balance and stay on course. In effect, keeping the head steady in its orientation to the horizon while the torso danced left and right was functionally equivalent to repeatedly turning the head left and right while the torso remained steady. That ability to turn the head and maintain balance was essential to the persistence runner's ability to chase down other animals, thereby reinforcing the abilities to endure and envision that were the precursors to invention and civilization building. Meanwhile, by the end of a two- or three-hour run on rough ground, the neck muscles had had almost as much of a workout as the legs.

So, as I glanced at the sun up behind me a bit west of the zenith, my neck was noticeably sore—thanks to the Appalachian Trail, no doubt. But that glance had also been triggered by the demand for another, equally critical, kind of balance—in my internal temperature. The running body burns calories relentlessly—first the glycogen already in the muscles or delivered from the liver; then the high-calorie replenishment you carry or pick up at aid stations, to the extent that you can assimilate it fast enough; and then body fat. If you go long enough even to deplete the fat, like one of Joseph Stalin's gulag-bound prisoners forced to march across Siberia in winter (whose calories were also being burned to keep him from dying of hypothermia), then the body begins cannibalizing itself—consuming its own muscle for fuel. When it does that, it is doing what our industrial economy has been doing for the past century—spending down the planet's finite resources. A runner will do well *not* to follow the example of the industrial economy.

The interconnectedness of all things (foot bone, knee bone; head turning, persistence hunting; envisioning, civilization building) never ceased to amaze me, sometimes with delightful and enlightening revelations, but other times with moments of sheer head-shaking chagrin. Body temperature, for example, "connects" not only to the obvious function of maintaining energy-use efficiency (not having to steal blood from the legs in order to keep the critical organs functioning on a freezing day, etc.), but also to not-so-obvious things such as your ability to tie your shoes. One frigid winter day in Virginia, I had the unnerving experience of having one of my shoelaces come untied in the middle of a race—the Swinging Bridge 50K, if I recall. This *never* happens to me; I always double-bow my laces. But in this race the course followed a little-used path through heavy undergrowth, and a vine or something must have gotten tangled with the lace and pulled it loose. I stopped to tie it, and—lo—my fingers, despite the gloves, were too frozen to grip the lace. Most of the blood had abandoned my fingers to do more important work inside, and the little finger muscles were helpless. I had to put my hands inside my shirt and under my armpits to warm them for a while, and it must have been ten minutes before I could finally get the shoe tied. Such a little thing! It was like another of those folk-wisdom proverbs about connection: For want of a shoe . . . the kingdom was lost.

So, cold can be a runner's adversary. But then, so can heat. Excessive heat, too, shunts blood and consumes calories. If it's a hot day, some of the blood may have to be diverted from the working muscles to carry heat to your face and neck (where the carotid artery brings heat very close to the surface) or to other unclothed surfaces, to get rid of it via evaporative or convective cooling. And then, too, the muscles—getting less blood and therefore less oxygen and fuel—have to work harder to keep up the same pace. Efficiency falls. And if it falls far enough, you fall too.

I was now around thirty-three miles into the race, with new challenges no doubt awaiting me like trolls, and I couldn't help recalling—with wistful bemusement—all those times I'd heard it said, and in fact said myself, that one of the great appeals of running is its simplicity. In 1977, extolling the virtues of running in one of the first issues of *Running Times*, I wrote: "As the world gets more complicated, people become more appreciative of the things that remain simple—and few things do. Running is in some ways the simplest of all sports. All you have to do, to run, is open the door and go out." And then there were all those little encouragements you'd hear from people encouraging their girlfriends or husbands or coworkers to give running a try: "Just put one foot in front of the other! It's that simple!"

I now understood that while that wasn't really wrong, it was far from the whole story. As an editor working for scientists, I learned very well how profoundly appealing—but also how much like a mirage—the notion of simplicity can be to anyone searching for answers. For scientists, simplicity is the holy grail of research. If a theory is too complicated, it is suspect. And if a phenomenon can be well explained by a very simple theory that has no contorted equations or loose ends, that theory is described as "elegant." In the workaday world of real research, though, science is rarely simple and never final. Running is simple to behold, no doubt in part because it has been honed by a hundred millennia of evolution. In look and feel, it can indeed be elegant. Yet scientists like Carrier, Bramble, Lieberman, and Heinrich—and scores of others—had by now devoted thousands of days to studying the biomechanics, physiology, anthropology, and neurology of this simplest of human activities, and the complexities only continued to grow.

From my own limited perspective, informed by my work with the ecology of the human footprint writ large, I knew that while energy *supply* was not the whole story for either a sustainable society or an enduring individual, energy *efficiency*—though a far bigger factor than most people thought—wasn't the whole story either. In my mouth, I still had a taste of the potato I'd picked up at Snyder's Landing— it's amazing how long it can take me to chew and swallow a bit of solid food when I'm running and breathing through my mouth—and that taste represented a disconcerting prospect for the miles ahead. I was a very tired sixty-year-old man, and even the most elementary math said that neither new energy supply nor the most highly efficient use of the little energy I had could possibly keep me going this way for another three hours. I had to find a way, and then it struck me: That last taste of potato in my mouth might offer a clue.

10

A BOILED-POTATO MIRACLE

Burning Fat in a Carbohydrate Fire:
A Secret of the Inca Messengers

THE IMPLICATIONS OF the energy-efficiency secret for human physiology, as well as for the human economy at large, were huge. I knew that, in endurance training, refueling too readily would be counterproductive, though this is what some athletic energy-supplement companies—echoing their fossil-fuel brethren—were suggesting. If the runner's body came to rely on constant new supply, it would not be compelled to adapt to greater efficiency in the use of a very limited supply. Again, the trick was *balance.* In training (as opposed to racing), you don't want to let yourself run out of fuel totally, but you do need to make yourself adapt to running farther with less. Then, when you race, you have both optimal supply *and* optimal efficiency, which should produce a better performance than just one or the other.

At Snyder's Landing, half an hour earlier, looking for my potato, I felt a bit like a vegan dinner guest eyeing the

Thanksgiving turkey dinner at his meat-loving cousin's home. The aid-station crews at the JFK 50 Mile have a friendly competition each year to see which crew can give the runners the greatest support and encouragement (the one at Taylor's, the station coming up next at mile 38, called itself the "38 Special"), and the resulting spread laid out on the tables looked to me like excess, although maybe that was just me.

Recalling the stop at Snyder's reminded me of an ultra I had run in Italy a few years ago, called the 100km del Passatore, where over ten thousand people had participated— about a third of them running, the others hiking. Ultras are much bigger in Europe, where maybe the culture isn't quite as frantic and workaholic as in the US and more people take time for slow pleasures. The Del Passatore had started in the main square of Florence, later in the day than most American races do, then climbed up and over the Apennine Mountains through the evening and night. Along the way, we passed villages where people had set up encampments by the roadside to offer us a continuous repast of Northern Italian cuisine— sausage-and-prosciutto pie, beef carpaccio, pine-nut-stuffed dates, pork-stuffed pasta, and ample wine. Village after village, it never ended, and if some of the hikers behind us had wished, they could have arrived at the Roman ceramics-making city of Faenza, where a large reception awaited us for the finish, completely drunk. There was a place in life, I could see, for long hikes with good food and wine. But not if you wanted to run like a persistence hunter.

In my marathon-running days, I often passed up refueling altogether, depending on that adapt-to-limited-fuel training strategy to get by with just the glycogen already stored in my muscles and liver when I went to the starting line. When I first tried ultras, I unthinkingly assumed the same strategy would work. It didn't. At least *some* refueling is needed if you go beyond your glycogen limit, which for most marathoners seems to be somewhere around twenty to twenty-two miles. What I would eventually learn is that just as there is an enormous leap of capacity as you shift from sprint metabolism to aerobic metabolism, there's another large leap that can be taken from marathon-range efficiency to the kind that can enable a well-trained man or woman to keep running for twenty-four hours, or even ten days, with only the briefest stops. At this level, humans can outlast horses or wolves. What happens is that, with proper training and fueling, the body shifts from burning carbohydrates as the primary fuel to relying more strongly on fat. Paradoxically, ultrarunners have (and need to have) less body fat than most other people—yet the little we have is of great value. Fat is the ultrarunner's secret friend.

I had learned about this in two stages—one brutal, the other easy. In the first, a little before I turned fifty, I ran the Angeles Crest 100 Mile over a very rugged part of the San Gabriel Mountains and reached complete exhaustion at seventy miles, where there was a big aid station at the foot of Mt. Wilson. The next four miles would be an unrelenting climb to the top of the mountain. How do you run up Mt. Wilson after running seventy miles over other mountains? I collapsed onto an army cot, nauseated at the very sight of water or food, my stomach in rebellion, my glycogen and blood sugar both long exhausted, wondering how in the world to refuel short of an intravenous injection. After about half an hour of introspection, it suddenly came to me that there was one thing I *could* eat without hurling—a boiled potato! And while I couldn't stand water, I could drink tea! Like a quarterback throwing a Hail Mary pass, I had gone *deep* with the Sheehan mantra—*listen to your body*—and an answer had come! I asked a volunteer if by any chance in the world they might have a boiled potato and some tea, and to my amazement they did. Evidently others had made this discovery before me. And thank heaven for aid station workers. I ate the potato, drank two cups of the tea, got to my feet, toddled out to the trail, and slowly worked my way from a lurch to a jog. And then, miraculously, I ran the final thirty miles on what could not have been more than ten potato-fueled calories per mile. I knew I'd have to be violating the laws of physics to do that on less than around 130 calories per mile. At the finish in the Rose Bowl, I was thrilled but mystified.

The second phase in my edification took only a minute, although it didn't happen until a couple of years later, when I mentioned my mystification about the potato to a veteran Virginia ultrarunner, Tom Corris. Tom smiled and told me about a phrase he'd heard from runners who studied exercise physiology: "Fat burns in a carbohydrate fire." Through a complex process, a small amount of carbohydrate can act as a kind of catalyst to facilitate the burning of fat, which is almost always in good supply in the body. In short, if you're well trained, you don't need to supply your body with another five thousand calories of fuel to go another five thousand calories' worth of distance; you may only need three hundred calories, *if* it's a form of carbohydrate your stomach can stand and *if* you've done enough long-distance training to adapt your metabolism so it will use that carbohydrate to ignite the energy-rich fat you already have. No matter how admirably lean you might be, unless you are actually starving, you still have enough fat to go for days. And what the carbohydrate does for that fat is like what kindling does for an oak log. At the Angeles Crest 100, I now understood, that little potato had set free my inner hunter. Back there at Snyder's Landing, I had thought, I don't *want* a feast. But I sure could use a boiled potato.

Some months after my conversation with Tom Corris, I found a Web site that provided a physiological explanation that did not just rely on a kindling-and-oak log analogy. It was from the American Council on Exercise:

> Fat burns in the flame of glucose, meaning that fat can only enter the mitochondrial energy pathways when there is enough of the end-product of glucose catabolism—pyruvic acid—along with oxygen, also present in the muscle cells. One of the key physiological adaptations of improved aerobic fitness is an enhanced capacity to utilize stored fat for ATP production. Functionally, it means that the lactate threshold is not reached until a much higher absolute intensity (caloric expenditure) is reached. This allows for more intense, as well as long duration, aerobic exercise.[1]

Translation: When you're running under normal conditions, some of the carbohydrate you consume breaks down to a substance (pyruvic acid) that then enters tiny power plants (mitochondria) within the muscle cells, where it meets up with the oxygen you inhale to convert the fat and other nutrients you've consumed into carbon dioxide and water—exhalation and sweat—thereby releasing energy. In this process, the nutrients are all broken down into a molecule called adenosine triphosphate (ATP), which is the immediate driver of muscular contraction. If you're exhausted and all you've got left in those tiny power plants is fat, you still need some of that pyruvic acid to turn it into ATP. A little carbo intake can keep those millions of power plants firing.

A coda to my Angeles Crest story: One day not long ago I learned a little more about the Chasquis, those mountain-running messengers of the ancient Incas whose territory spanned the Peruvian Andes *where wild potatoes grew*. When the Chasquis were on the run, it seems, wild potatoes were their primary fuel. The potatoes provided the glucose that produced the pyruvic acid that combined with that Andean mountain air to produce the ATP that kept them on the move.

■ ■ ■

A few hundred yards ahead, I noticed a guy running without a shirt. The air was still cold, but running generates a lot of heat. And some men (I'm always conscious of how unfair this is to women, who aren't granted the same freedom) take off their shirts whenever it gets even a little warm. While heat buildup may be what the guys think they're responding to, I think there's something else as well. In the evolution of awareness, one of the key developments was an epochal movement from the very hairy body of an ape to the bare skin of a modern human. To a human, *naked* means more than just "without clothes," in the sense that a dog or bear is without clothes. Feeling the sun and air on our bare skin can have a powerful hold on us. Some of that traces to implied sexuality, in the same way that our ability to envision the future may trace to hunting the not-physically-visible prey that has disappeared around the bend ahead. But there's another powerful trace as well.

In their gradual migration from the shade of forest canopy to the hot sunlight of open grassland, our hominid ancestors had to make tremendous physical adaptations. Yes, they may have had to get up on two limbs in order to see over the high grass, or in order to free the other two limbs to carry weapons or water or their babies. At the same time, though, they no doubt had to adapt to the consequences both of being out in open sunlight and of traversing much longer distances than they had ever traveled as apes. Fast walking—and eventually, running—generates a lot of heat. The body of a runner, like the engine of a car, has to get rid of waste heat as rapidly as it's generated, or else fail.

I learned this the easy way, by running in a temperate, East Coast climate. One January in Philadelphia, for example, I ran a twenty-mile race during a blizzard. The air was below freezing, and I wore a hooded sweatshirt and shorts. A photographer for the Philadelphia *Evening Bulletin*, happening to see me go by, considered my bare legs enough of a curiosity in this driving snow to take a picture, which appeared on the front page of the next day's paper—and then was reprinted on an inside page the following day, along with the caption "Who Is He?"—as if I were some extraterrestrial who didn't understand *cold*. But, in fact, I understood it well enough to know that if I wore a hood over my head (which is a major heat-radiator) in order to keep my ears from freezing, I needed some other part of my body to serve as an efficient radiator. Running at a rate of about six minutes per mile, I was generating enough heat that the cold air on my legs nicely balanced the high heat output.

If I tried to run at that pace on a hot African savanna, the challenge would be much harder. I would have to cope not only with the heat generated by my metabolism, but also that of the sun's direct radiation on me. But that's where the real adaptive genius of *naked skin* comes into play. The human body, as presently configured, has not just one cooling mechanism, but three. A car has a radiator. But a man or woman in motion, in addition to radiating heat directly, can also cool by convection, which is the transfer of heat by the *movement* of skin against air or of air against skin (the "breeze" effect), and by evaporation of sweat. The convection and evaporation work much more effectively with bare skin than with heavy hair or fur. One of the reasons we humans are among the most enduring of all large animals is that we *are* so naked. Give us sufficient water to keep sweating, and we can run for a very long time without overheating. Our nakedness was one of the keys to our ability to outrun woolly mammoths, given enough time to let the heat in the bigger animal build up.

When a three-year-old mischievously flings off all his clothes and runs across the lawn or beach, he's not just being mischievous; he's getting at least a fleeting sense of something quite primal in his human nature. The child is probably hardwired to feel pleasure in the movement of air on skin. I know it's true for me. And if this pleasure is innate, I suspect the reason is that this direct contact of skin with air is part of a larger set of contacts between body and environment that were selected for their capacity to provide critical *information*, as well as to provide cooling or other homeostatic services. The selection was reinforced by pleasure, and eventually by the conscious *prospect* of pleasure. Other parts of this information-gathering system include the feel of bare feet on earth (vestiges of which are often enjoyed by gardeners or beachgoers, as well as by some runners), and all the other sensory or kinesthetic connections that still affect what we like or don't like.

I know we now regard our "nature-loving" likes and dislikes as mainly aesthetic preferences. We like the smell of pine forests and the sound of birds on a summer morning but don't consider them critical to our ability to thrive or survive. Once, though, they were. In 1964, the psychologist Erich Fromm coined the phrase *biophilia* to refer to the human "love of life" or "love of living systems." Twenty years later, the biologist Edward O. Wilson collaborated with Stephen Kellert on a book called *The Biophilia Hypothesis*, in which they argued that the human love of nature is in fact hardwired, an artifact of our evolution in an environment where trees, flowers, waterfalls, other animals, and the sun and moon were matters of survival, not just enjoyable to look at. Our contact with nature was what kept us alive. And more pertinent to our present condition, this contact was also critical to our capacity to *think*—to make observations, inferences, projections, and plans that could successfully compensate for our lack of physical speed, power, and sharp claws or teeth.

A lot of animals evolved mainly through blind adaptation. We didn't. When we felt the breeze pass across our nostrils and chests, we were already envisioning what awaited us far ahead on the trail or over the horizon. And now, when some of us enjoy visiting a wild place with a spectacular vista, or living in a house with a great view, we may be reconnecting with that evolutionary journey we took from *vision* on the trail to *envisioning* what was around the bend ahead to becoming the *visionary species* that can actually choose the course of its own future.

The guy up ahead of me, bare chest to the chill wind, might have looked a little crazy to a casual passerby—though on this part of the trail there was really no one to notice. If he was still shirtless when we hit the road after Dam Number 4, people in passing cars would probably shake their heads. The temperature now felt like low-fifties, and the windchill felt lower. On the other hand, it also seemed to me that half of the runners I'd seen since we came off the AT were overdressed—still wearing the windbreakers or long-sleeve shirts they'd started out with at dawn.

Temperature management is one of the trickiest skills a runner can learn. I learned when I was younger that if you're running fairly fast, the body generates so much heat that to keep at optimal strength you often need to be more lightly clad than you expected when you stepped out the door. And I still recalled, though it now seemed hard for my aging body to believe, that when I was running marathons in the 1960s and '70s, I decided that the perfect temperature for running a marathon (assuming you're wearing shorts and a singlet) was about forty-nine degrees Fahrenheit. Years later, the US Army Research Institute of Medicine would do a study of energy efficiency in runners over a range of temperatures and conclude that the ideal temperature is forty-one degrees Fahrenheit. Of course, that's an average. A very lean runner with a higher-than-average surface-to-volume ratio (more skin area per pound, and less distance for the blood to carry heat to the skin) is more efficient at cooling, and may have a slightly higher ideal temperature, while a bigger person might do better when it's cooler. That guy up ahead might actually be right on target. And the rest of us might be a little too desensitized by the same cultural separation from our world that was making us unresponsive to the steadily thickening blanket of carbon dioxide over our warming earth.

I thought of the story ecologists tell, about the frog and the pot of water. Drop a frog into a pot of boiling water, they say, and it will jump out. Put it in a pot of cold water and then gradually heat it to a boil, and it will remain in the pot until it is dead. I'd never actually tried that and didn't plan to. But I did wonder, at times when I began to feel the heat building up under my shirt, whether I wouldn't really rather be running naked, the way our persistence-hunting ancestors did. And I wondered how long we humans will let ourselves cook before we *do* wake up and jump.

I recalled an article I'd written for *Running Times* in 1980. For some reason, I could still remember the first line: "The last weekend of Henry Kronlage's life was, until very near the end, a happy one."[2]

Henry Kronlage was a forty-five-year-old, moderately experienced road runner who in August of that year signed up to run the Herndon 10 Mile run in the Washington, DC, suburb of Herndon, Virginia. The previous month had been the hottest month in a hundred years in that region. On the day of the race, the air at the start had been stifling. But Kronlage was in a jubilant mood, as his whole family was together that weekend and two of his kids—fifteen-year-old Lynn and thirteen-year-old Karl—were entered in the race, too. A few days before, Henry had kidded his son, "The first time you stop for water, I'll pass you!"[3]

Lynn later recalled that during the run she struggled with the heat, and in the last mile she felt dizzy and began to wobble. At the finish she was close to collapsing. She slumped to the ground, and fortunately someone poured cold water on her. In a previous race, she had not been happy to reach the finish and find that her dad had finished ahead of her (he was waiting there to cheer her), but now, when she really needed him, he wasn't there. After the race, no one knew where he was. Another man was also missing. It wasn't until two days later that the body of Henry Kronlage was found in some bushes a short distance from the finish line. The course had taken a right-angle turn a few hundred yards from the finish, marked by a chalk arrow on the pavement, but there was no sentry, and Kronlage—dizzied by heatstroke—missed the turn. Finding no finish line or relief, he apparently went into the bushes seeking shade, and no one was there to pour cold water on him.

As it happened, the other missing man died in that race, too. My story focused on Kronlage but also became an inquiry into what went wrong when 500 runners went to the starting line and only 498 reached the finish alive. If I thought there was a simple answer, though, I was soon disabused. Henry Kronlage had taken off his shirt at the start, so he wasn't overdressed. But a lot of other factors came into play. The runners had to walk half a mile from the parking area to the starting line on hot pavement in full sun. The race started at 9:15 AM with the temperature at ninety-five degrees. The entire ten miles was on heat-radiating pavement with no shade. The stricken runners were both in their forties, the significance of which was suggested to me by Dale Hruby, an officer at the nearby National War College at Fort McNair. Hruby was a veteran runner whose job was to prepare senior military officers and government officials—mostly men between thirty-five and forty-five—to take on higher levels of responsibility, including responsibility for their own physical condition. He told me he had become "acutely conscious of how intensely competitive men in their 30s and 40s often become, especially when matched up with younger rivals."[4]

That race, and its aftermath, became a turning point in the management of long-distance races in America. Phil Stewart, one of my partners at the magazine, had photographed the race and later launched a spinoff publication, *Road Race Management*, which would help to build critical expertise in the planning of running events. Courses would rarely, thereafter, go over unshaded roads in summer heat; summer races would start at 6:00 or 7:00 AM or in the evening, instead of at mid-morning; medical personnel would be on hand; race officials would be trained to recognize the symptoms of heat exhaustion or stroke; right-angle turns would have sentries. And the management of running events needed to be handled by people who were, themselves, experienced runners.

About a month after the Herndon race, we received a

letter from a man who'd been watching the Tennessee state high school cross-country championship in which his son was competing. He'd overheard someone saying something about "a runner staggering around," and at first thought nothing of it. But then, he wrote, he remembered the article we'd published on "The Herndon Tragedy," and particularly the statement that "we are a fellowship responsible to each other." So he and a photographer friend began searching, and persisted at it, longer than they normally might have. Eventually, they found a boy lying in an out-of-the-way ditch, "comatose with dry hot skin exhibiting papillary signs, etc.— a victim of heat stroke."[5] The writer wanted us to know that that reminder about the fellowship of runners and their supporters had helped save the boy's life.

Decades later, I came across that letter again, by then long forgotten, and from the perspective of a now-older man it seemed to me that "searching" is really what endurance running has been about from the beginning. Hunter-gatherers searched for food, whether it was growing in the forest or running on four legs across the savanna. As climate changed, they migrated and searched for better hunting grounds. And as the neurology of envisioning developed, they searched for ways of not just adapting to their environment but reshaping it.

And now, I thought, we need to search for ways of restoring some of the balances we have upset. In the late stages of a race, it is clarifying to know that the quest for balance, even more than for speed, is my guide. If an athlete gets complacent in the late stages of a competition, it can all collapse. Whether I'm a sixty-year-old man contemplating the last stage of his life or an ultrarunner in the last stage of a race, it's critical to keep searching. You never know what you'll find around the next bend and what help from the fellowship you might need.

A BOILED-POTATO MIRACLE

11

TAYLOR'S LANDING

Negotiating with Fatigue—and
Turning Long Hours into Moments

A COUPLE OF hours ago, I had managed to find the slow-the-game wormhole and calm the turmoil within. And periodically, I had replenished enough carbs to keep even the fat of an ectomorphic sixty-year-old burning. But now a new challenge—the kind of fatigue that even smart fueling and a Zen state of equanimity can't dispel—was making itself known. I didn't even need Sheehan's mantra to hear the message my body was telling me now: *This is getting old.* A part of it, inexorably, was that I myself was getting old. I'd been running for forty-four years, and it felt like that entire span had been today, and I had maybe another twenty years to run before the day would be over.

I also had to pee, which seemed to be happening more often as I grew older. In my own variant of that getting-older joke about climbing stairs ("Have you noticed that stairs are getting steeper?"), I thought, "Have you noticed that they put

the porta-johns much farther apart now than they used to?"
So, with no official facility in sight, I stopped and stepped off
the towpath right where I was, which is what ultrarunners do
in most races anyway. It doesn't matter whether other runners pass by as you do. They'll have to take their turns, too.
Out on the trail, those kinds of inhibitions no longer matter.

My pee wasn't quite the hue of a sunset yet, which meant
at least I wasn't dangerously dehydrated. If the urine is fairly
clear, let's say lemonade color or lighter, you are probably
getting enough water. If it's dark, you really need to drink. I
stepped back to the path, ready to resume running, but unfortunately the fatigue was still with me. Fatigue holds you in
its grip and doesn't get pissed off. In fact, it's quite friendly
and only wants you to be more comfortable. It wants you to
stop and lie down, for God's sake. So what should I do?

If I had come to an impasse like this a few decades ago, I
might well have considered stopping at Taylor's Landing, not
far from here now, and waiting for the sweeper truck that
picks up every runner who doesn't reach a designated check-
point by the cutoff time for that point. I was still hours ahead
of the cutoff for Taylor's, but fatigue doesn't care what time
it is—and it won't hesitate to tell you that, if you would like,
you can always just tell yourself *this is stupid*, sit down, and
close your eyes until the hours pass, which will be quickly
enough.

But experience at least gave me a way to escape the grim
sweeper. The most useful thing for a competitive runner to
know about fatigue is that it is fundamental to nature. *Fatigue
is not an enemy*, and if you fight it as if it were, you squander
what little energy you still have. Better to think of fatigue the
way you might think of evaporation if you were on a long trek
across the Kalahari Desert. The evaporation of your sweat
dehydrates you, and if you ignore it you can die. But

evaporation is also what cools you enough to keep you alive, if you work with it. It's a very big part of what made you human to begin with. It's what made your ancestors able to catch bison and eat grass-fed steak.

Needless to say, by this point in my life I'd had a fairly costly education not only in fuels and efficiency, but in the nature of fatigue itself. That education had come via some arduous experiences with marathons and ultras, but also via my editing work on the fragility of ecosystems. In the larger world, everything wears out in time. If it were true, as biologists like Harvard's Edward O. Wilson had calculated, that 99.9 percent of all the species that had ever lived on the earth had gone extinct, one could think of those extinctions as a form of terminal fatigue on the Darwinian field of battle. And if that was true, then our own species' rush to seek risky shortcuts in our civilization's progress could only cause our collective exhaustion to come faster. We replace highly complex ecosystems with monoculture, for example. Ecological balances are quickly upset; the soil is depleted; crops fail; the empire falls. It's like a runner taking a shortcut in a race, which defeats the whole meaning of *having* a race. In an evolutionary eyeblink, we have discovered—as Ted Taylor and some of his Los Alamos colleagues did when they grew a little older and wiser—that it's not smart to try to out-create our own Creator, at least not when, as a species, we are still in our adolescence.

But did any of this rather fatalistic view help me cope with my own very immediate fatigue? In one respect, it did. In pondering the histories of human institutions, I had seen a common, almost predictable, pattern: As our institutions grow older, they become more fixed in their ways—less flexible (like the calves or quads of an aging athlete), less resilient, less responsive to the kinds of creative inspiration that led to their founding and early growth. The fresh spirit of a young Jesus, with his message of compassion and forgiveness and outrage at the moneylenders in the temple, had somehow transmogrified, over the centuries, into the punitive doctrines of a rich and powerful global church. The fresh spirit of a young nation with its declaration of equal opportunity for all had transmogrified into an intercontinental enterprise that trafficked in slaves, killed hundreds of thousands of natives, and incarcerated its Japanese citizens. And as institutions became more rigid, they also became more vulnerable to cracking and breaking up—whether via religious schisms or civil wars. It occurred to me that maybe the most effective way to fend off institutional fatigue or collapse, and to bring rejuvenating life and energy, is not to further tighten the grip of an institution on the hardened rules and ideologies that define it now, but to regenerate some of the creative spirit that formed it in the beginning. And if that can work, then maybe the greatest function of idealism is *not* to guide the way to a utopian outcome, as we habitually assume, but to help us reinvigorate or re-create our institutions when they have grown weary. Utopias never happen, but revolutions and rebirths sometimes do.

The implications for my running—for that one realm of life where I had some real control of outcomes and opportunity to build strength and spirit—had been an epiphany. An important part of my training experience—maybe the *quintessential* part—had been the very occasional times when I would hit a stretch of running that felt magical. I called these my "forever" runs, because any sense of gradually tiring was gone; I was in a timeless zone, experiencing a sense that I could run like this forever. I had always assumed that the value of these rare moments was to help prepare me for the day when I could run like that in a race. But now I understood—this was the revelation—that the real value of these in-the-zone moments was in practicing the kind of feeling I'd need to bring into play *not* when I'm headed for a fantastic performance but when I'm struggling with deep fatigue or discouragement.

I had learned enough about physiology to be aware that feelings have powerful biochemical impacts. We've all heard stories about the ninety-eight-pound woman who sees her child pinned under a car and in a surge of primal emotion lifts the rear end of the car clear off the ground to save the child. Maybe those stories are urban myths, but I believe it has happened. I don't know whether it's epinephrine or endorphins or the sudden bushwhacking of new neural pathways or what, but something happens.

I was in the no-man's-land between Snyder's Landing and Taylor's Landing, still with over a half-marathon to go, and I needed something to happen. The "forever" feeling, if I could conjure it up, might be that something. I have never given much credence to the cliché of the "runner's high" because it seems backward to me—like magical thinking. The real high doesn't pop up like a quick, assured consequence of running. It isn't like effortlessly popping Prozac or smoking marijuana. Rather, going out to run, day after day, if you did it long enough, would very occasionally produce that high like a hard-earned reward. You had to really work for it. And it was paradoxical, because while I called it a "forever" feeling, it was in truth only a moment in time.

The idea of a "moment in time" has become fairly central to my understanding of endurance running—what it really is and how it works. It fascinates me that nonrunners so often seem to think that running long distances must be intolerably boring. "What do you *think* about when you're running?" they ask. In a way, this question is quite understandable, because we've been conditioned by our culture to be more and more dependent on distraction, as if we are constitutionally unable to entertain ourselves. Doctors' waiting rooms have to have the TV on constantly, because otherwise the patients would have no idea what to do with themselves. The doctors would have to add "cabin fever" to everyone's chart! And, of course, we have that culturally manufactured demand for quick reward. I've noticed that for most of my lifetime, TV coverage of the Olympics has given a lot of attention to the sprints, but very little to the distance events. Viewers can watch the 100 meters and get a thrill in just ten seconds, and the 400 meters in well under a minute—although that seems to be about as long as the producers want to go without a break. But the longer events make the producers balk. John Parker, who was assigned by a New York magazine to review the TV coverage of the 1984 Olympics, later recalled in his book *Runners & Other Dreamers* that ABC gave plenty of attention to the sprinter Carl Lewis ("There was a tendency to 'Lewis' us to death"), but that the 5,000 meters, which was run at 7:30 PM that Saturday night, and which the great miler Marty Liquori would later call "the greatest 5,000 ever run," was not aired by the network until about 2:00 AM Eastern time. Rather than show that distance event when people might still be awake, they showed a handball game between Yugoslavia and West Germany. *Anything* but ask a primetime American audience to watch an event that might drag on for thirteen whole minutes! And as for the 10,000 meters— Parker watched in vain and eventually suspected that the network had managed not to show that event at all.[1]

So, if minute after minute of running is hard to watch, what about hour after hour? And what about the poor souls who are actually *doing* it? That question of what we long-distance runners "think about" during those long hours on the road or trail has been occasionally explained as a fundamental difference between what experienced runners do when racing or engaging in training runs expressly intended to practice racing conditions, and the more easygoing runs people do just for fitness or fun, or to build a "base" to prepare your body for more ambitious workouts weeks later. When racing, the runner is like an airplane pilot (before the days of autopilot and drones) who is fully engaged in monitoring and adjusting the controls. In this so-called associative mode, the runner is monitoring and adjusting his breathing, heart rate, core temperature, hydration, perspiration, tempo, gait, available energy, electrolyte level, nutrient intake, flirtation with anaerobic or lactate threshold, and of course the conditions of his ambient environment: air temperature and humidity, precipitation, wind velocity and direction, and terrain—and anticipation of the road ahead. Some of it is done subconsciously and some with deep attentiveness.

On a more easygoing (or dissociative) run, he might think about his work or family, or replay a recent conversation in his head, or imagine what he'd *like* to have said in that conversation—or he might notice the wildlife around him with the same appreciation he would when going for a walk in Rock Creek Park or a hike in Yellowstone, or he might chat with a running partner about whether the Cubs will ever win the World Series.

That's what runners think about on a long run: sometimes a continuous stream of data about the running itself, and other times a stream of anything from profundity to trivia about whatever.

That's the conventional dichotomy: associative running and dissociative running. But I have another perspective, too—not a contradiction of that conventional dichotomy, but a different perspective on the *real* question being asked by the nonrunner. When someone asks "What do you think about?" what I think he or she is really getting at is: *How do you make the time pass?*

The answer, I eventually realized, is that it actually passes in brief, vivid moments. *Moments* are what make up the character of either a lifetime or a long-distance run, not endless days or hours. I have no idea whether every minute I've ever lived—or spent on the road or trail—is actually recorded somewhere deep in my brain. Once in a while, something will pop into my consciousness after decades, and I'm surprised to discover that it was there all along. But I really don't care whether it's the tip of a Freudian iceberg or just a random fragment floating in a mostly empty storage space.

What *is* important to me is a relatively small number of moments that I will always remember, whether in my running or in life at large. The rest is chaff. And what's truly curious is that these moments add up to only a very small amount of time. If you asked me what I recalled of the past three hours of this run, the truth is that most of it was by now a blank. I recalled my kiss with Sharon at Keep Tryst . . . those few seconds of watching Frank Probst with his head bent over . . . the crowds at Weverton and Antietam ("Good job! Good job!") and then seeing the cliffs and recalling the story of Killiansburg Cave . . . and looking for a potato at Snyder's . . . and being passed by the young navy guy and the girl (that one might be a keeper) . . . and the Marine politely telling me I was bleeding (and saying "sir" to an old antiwar Quaker!—that one too a keeper). But all the actual moments I could consciously recall might add up to no more than twenty seconds.

And by the way, where *was* Frank now?

This reduction of a few hours to twenty seconds wasn't because I was getting old. My memory now was as good as it had ever been—I was terrible with names, good with mental maps and big-picture views of the world, and really good with musical tunes—and I really didn't know whether this distillation of time was genetic or cultural. It might have been conditioned by our entertainment media's emphasis on highlights: sports highlights, news highlights, the high points of someone's life summarized in a seventy-five-word obituary. Whatever the explanation, I figured that if I made a list of the moments that made up the significant memories of my forty-four years of competitive running until now, I'd be surprised if they added up to more than ten minutes:

- **High school cross-country, sophomore year, 1956:** Riding to a meet in the bus, the guys loudly singing, "Bee-bop, ba-loo-la, She's my ba-by!" and bouncing around in their seats. Why remember this? Maybe it was my initiation into the ancient adventure of being part of a *band* of runners who depended on each other for survival and sustenance—the persistence-hunting band.

- **High school track, same year:** Passing Tom Sisko, the school's ace distance runner, on the last turn of the fourth lap, on the way to a 4:49 mile. Passing Tom Sisko! Actually passing him took about three seconds. That mile took 289 seconds to run, but I can only remember those three.

- **Swarthmore College cross-country:** Flying over a section of the home course in Crum Woods that was treacherously rocky and rooty, but that I felt I knew so well that I could run over it without fear. I broke the course record on that day, but have no memory of the finish—only of flying over those rocks and roots. Ten seconds at most.

- **Road running, 1970-something:** Out in front of that twenty-mile race in a blizzard in Philadelphia, the snow blowing against my face and bare legs, feeling strong. Just a flash of a moment, like a photo.

- **Mountain trail, California, early summer:** On an easy training run along a ridge near the Leona Divide, I came to a very narrow section of trail where dead scrub-oak leaves had accumulated along the edge of the path. My left foot came down almost on top of a rattlesnake, which had been well camouflaged by the leaves. I may even have grazed it. I had always wondered what would happen if I stepped on a rattlesnake on the run. Which would be faster, the strike of the snake or the movement of my striding leg away from its reach? What happened here—my mind slowed the game and although it took only a fraction of a second, I saw it in clear detail—was that the snake, caught by surprise and not coiled, thrashed left and right looking for its assailant, and by then my leg was in the clear. I can still replay that moment and see the snake thrashing and hear its sudden rattling. A fraction of one second.

- **The US 50 Mile Championship, New York City, 1976:** Rounding the last bend of the Central Park loop course, seeing the finish banner a few hundred yards ahead and knowing that if I could hold my place I'd win the bronze medal—a national championship medal! Here, for the first time in twenty years of running and with that banner in sight, I broke a rule I'd always dutifully observed—*Don't look back!* Maybe coaches had started hectoring their runners about that after that dramatic moment in the British Empire Games of 1954 when Roger Bannister and John

Landy dueled in an epic mile that was heard on radio by a hundred million people worldwide. Track was big that year. Bannister was the first man to break the four-minute barrier, but Landy soon became the second, dramatically breaking Bannister's world record. On the last turn of the showdown, Landy was ahead by a step. He looked over his left shoulder to see where Bannister was—and as he turned his head, Bannister darted past his blind spot on the right to seize the one-stride lead he needed to win. It was the ambush heard around the world—because Landy had looked back. But for me, what mattered now was not just holding third place but capturing the moment as I did it. I didn't want to wait until I crossed the finish line to know that I had, incredibly, beaten the guy behind me, Steve Molnar, even though Molnar could probably outsprint me if he was close. Molnar had recently done a 2:22 marathon, nine minutes faster than my PR, and not bad for those days. But on this day I'd passed him right around the marathon point, twenty-three miles back, and I wasn't going to capitulate to any fear of being taken by surprise, not now! I wanted to feel the thrill the whole last two hundred yards to the finish and have that to keep. So I looked back to see: Was Molnar there? And he wasn't. It turned out that he was less than two minutes behind me, just out of sight around the last bend, but that was enough: From around that bend, even Roger Bannister couldn't have caught me now. And ever after, I would be glad I'd finally broken that rule, because that would prove to be the fastest ultra I ever ran. And on my mental book shelf, it would always have a special place. Out of the five hours and forty-six minutes it took me, what I remembered of it now—easing past Steve Molnar at around twenty-seven miles, then three hours later kicking into an endorphin high and running the final two hundred yards *feeling that whole last stretch forever*—added up to almost a minute.

There were other moments I'd kept. But out of forty-four years and perhaps twenty thousand hours of training and racing, the moments I carried consciously would probably add up to only a few minutes. I travel light.

That's not to say there aren't important categories of experiences in which hundreds of hours of training build judgment and skill. I specifically recalled only a couple of face-plants, the first one during a solo thirty-one miler on a hot summer day in the Catoctin Mountains of Maryland—not far from here, actually—where, as my hand instinctively flew forward to break the fall, the water bottle strapped to the hand hit the ground first and the lid popped off, splashing all my water into the dirt. Fortunately I rescued myself by finding a patch of ripe blueberries. The other face-plant was that one back at Weverton, three hours earlier in the race. But I'd had other falls I don't specifically remember, and hundreds of near-falls, all of which added to my skill.

During the past year of training for this JFK, I had developed a perspective regarding how the time passes that I knew could be useful—maybe even vital—in the final miles. The way I saw it, the hundreds of memorable moments that make up an individual lifetime, and the millions that make up the history of a civilization, constitute the very heart of a vital person or society. These are all moments of what Buddhists call "mindful" experience, in which you are fully *in the present*. These present moments are slowed or even captured to be with you forever, like that image of runners on an ancient Grecian urn—running and yet still there, at least until someone drops the urn! "When old age shall this generation waste, Thou shalt remain," John Keats wrote of such a captured moment, in his "Ode on a Grecian Urn."[2]

But of course, there are two other broad categories of captured time that pose a great challenge to how mental energy is used. Too often, "dwelling on the past" constitutes a huge waste of energy on regret, resentment, or emotional scarring that refuses to heal. And too often, apprehensions or fears about the future can inhibit or cripple one's capability to move strongly *into* the future. To selectively deploy the remembered highlights of past life as instructive inspiration or edification for future action, though, can add great strength to the effort. Likewise, to deploy well-guided anticipation of the course can help us to avert fateful stumbles and falls, the way our eye-brain coordination can look several strides down the trail and direct our feet faster than the conscious mind can decide where to put them.

Somewhere along the way, with still over four miles to go to Dam 4 and about a half-marathon to the finish, I tripped and stumbled briefly before catching my balance. The towpath out here had more fallen leaves on it than I'd seen back around Keep Tryst or Antietam—so maybe I tripped on a root. In a flash, I thought of the incredibly complex set of neurological responses that were put into play in just that one quick rebalancing. Maybe I was being just a bit too dissociative now, but I was reminded again of John Kennedy's conviction about how closely linked the brain and body must be. To avoid stumbles, whether momentary or monumental, was not just an autonomic physical balancing act, but a critical skill at connecting the mindful present with the remembered past and anticipated future. A few years after this race, I would learn that a major, multi-year study had been undertaken to measure the effects of cardiovascular fitness on intelligence. As reported by Futurity.org, a study of 1.2 million young men, conducted by Maria Alberg of the University of Gothenberg in Sweden and Nancy Pederson of the University of Southern California, found that boys who increased their cardiovascular fitness from ages fifteen to eighteen—by participating in cross-country running or skiing—scored significantly higher on tests of intelligence than those who didn't. Presumably, the same result would be found for girls. The authors found that "in every measure of cognitive functioning they analyzed— from verbal ability to logical performance to geometrical per- ception to mechanical skills—average scores increased according to aerobic fitness." The study was published in the *National Academy of Sciences Early Edition* in 2009.[3]

When I eventually learned about that study, I assumed that if it got any media attention at all (it might be a bit too sticky for editors to be comfortable with), the discussion would quickly focus on the implications for schools and standard- ized tests. But by the time of this JFK race, I was already in- clined to suspect that a far more important implication of the body/brain connection relates to how it affects our abilities to recover from stumbles—not just on rocks or roots, but over the barriers we have erected between ourselves and the future we have put in jeopardy. The mental capacities we need most now are more acute and far-reaching skills at see- ing what awaits us over the horizon or around the bends ahead.

12

DAM NUMBER 4

Seeing Around Bends: We Came, We
Envisioned . . . We Got Disconnected

THAT LAST FIVE miles of the towpath is the longest and loneli-
est five miles of the entire JFK 50—even longer, I guessed,
than the last miles on the road were going to seem after leaving the dam, because on the road I would at least sense the
finish edging closer. But out here on this remote stretch of
the river, I was no longer noticing any bicyclists or hikers
around, and the runners were ever farther apart, and the
minutes were feeling endless. Instead of the hours turning
into moments, they felt like months.

I was now watching vigilantly for the dam. This would be
one of the five dams that had been built in the early nineteenth century to divert water from the river to the C&O
Canal, and—like the land on either bank—had been fought
over in the Civil War. The next dam back down the river,
Number 5, if I wasn't mistaken, was the one that the Confederates had tried to blow up by planting explosives in its base

late one night. I had a faint memory of how Number 4 would appear around a long bend in the river, far ahead on the left: a pale blue-grey impressionist brushstroke across the water. Beyond my trick of remembering how *good* running can feel, two other things kept me going: envisioning that dam, and— well, patience. I know "patience" doesn't sound so much like a practiced skill as just an absence of urgency. But by now I knew that patience, far from being a willingness to go mentally slack, is in fact a form of deep attentiveness.

That kind of attentiveness could not be passive—it couldn't be like those half-asleep guards who keep getting ambushed in action movies. If I allowed anxiety to sneak up on me, it would go right to my gut. But if I could clearly identify the causes of the anxiety before it got to me, it would usually retreat—like a bad dream that fades when you open your eyes to the light of morning.

Waking up, to me, always meant a new beginning. So, that's what an embrace of patience was—a new beginning. It was a childlike look at the world with wide-open receptivity to whatever adventure was coming my way. I still have a memory— one of those moments that make up a lifetime—of kneeling in the woods near my childhood home in Berkeley Heights, New Jersey, staring in wonder at a jack-in-the-pulpit. I'd been told I must never pick one of those, and I never did. I stared at it for a minute, then *ran* back to the house to tell my mother what I'd found! Half a century later, I looked that place up on Google Maps and found that the spot where I'd knelt was now the middle of Interstate 78, a main route for trucks carrying cargo from Pennsylvania through the Holland Tunnel into New York. Within my lifetime, the astonishing ecology of those woods, which took hundreds of millennia to evolve, had been obliterated by my species and covered with the exhumed remains (asphalt) of even more ancient forests. My civilization was too impatient, and it was a struggle not to succumb to the urgency. But to get impatient at this point in a race, with a long way yet to go, would be a mistake. I don't have any quarrel with progress; I *like* true progress (I am a child of evolution!) and was trying to make good progress down the path, but not in a hell-bent way that would backfire.

So I now had to call on a mental trick I'd learned, a sort of new application of the Sheehan mantra: to regard any situation that tempts me to abandon my patience as a new beginning. *Listen again.* The impulse to get anxious or frustrated or angry, or to quit, is a thing that happens when you feel you should be very close to the end of something—like the long haul to this dam!—and not being there yet can lead to panicky or reckless decisions. I'd once read that prisoners are more likely to attempt an escape when their scheduled release is only days away than when they have many years left. The trick is to change the perspective and see the moment not as near-the-end but as a new beginning, like the moment when you're standing still at the starting line of a new race. Patience is rebirth.

I know this might sound like pop psychology, a trick of words. But the fact is, it was now past one o'clock in the afternoon and I'd been running for over six hours straight and hadn't yet fallen on my face (well okay, there'd been that one time on the AT, but I'd gotten back up), and arguably I couldn't still be out here, still *truckin'*, as we used to say in the '60s, if I hadn't actually had quite a few new beginnings. You can't just put the human body on cruise control and drift into a half-sentient state as if you were driving on I-78 at 3:00 AM. You have to be attentive, like that boy I once was, looking with wide-eyed wonder at that endangered jack-in-the-pulpit, or like a Buddhist or Quaker in meditation, who is very still and might even look asleep, but is deeply aware.

I had experienced new beginnings each time I passed a landmark on the course—at the South Mountain trailhead, at the turn from the unexplained service road back to the Appalachian Trail, at the start down the Weverton switchbacks, and each time I had departed from an aid station, reinvigorated by a good swig of water or electrolyte drink. Each time, it was a reminder to compose myself, quiet the turmoil, relax, get into rhythm, find perfect balance. That's *work!* But it's efficient work, consuming minimal mental or physical fuel. If done well, it leaves no idle hands, no energy to be squandered on anxiety.

Now, as I watched for the dam, I could see another dimension of patience as well—or maybe it was just the same dimension in another light. A few weeks prior to the race, I'd had a phone conversation with Bernd Heinrich, whose book *Racing the Antelope* had just been published. I don't recall Heinrich's exact words, but it was undoubtedly the memory of that conversation that had provoked the fantasy I'd had back on the AT about wondering if I might spot Heinrich himself, around one of the next bends on the trail. What I did recall was my realization that one of the signal attributes of the early persistence hunter had to have been his capacity to pursue an animal even when it had temporarily disappeared from sight. It also gave me an instant sense of recognition: When I'm competing in a trail race, an essential part of what sustains my motivation is the knowledge that when I go around the next bend into a long straightaway, I'll again catch sight of the guys I'm trying to catch. I can't see them right now, but *I know they're there.* Whereas a big cat might give up the chase fairly quickly after the quarry is no longer visible, the human would keep pursuing. This "out-of-sight but *not* out-of-mind" idea seemed to add a critical consideration to the running-man theory of our species' origins.

As a careful empirical scientist, Heinrich hesitated to speculate about what may have been in the minds of those persistence hunters. But it seems to me, as a latter-day hominid who has run several times the circumference of our planet and had ample time to let my mind run ahead of me, that what must have kept the early hunter pursuing when his eyes no longer saw the prey was some form of mental construct that temporarily substituted for the optical one—like the digital file of a photo. The first such constructs may have been faint and short-lived, like some mutant form of the dreaming we know other mammals do—incipient daydreams-on-the-run that proved over a thousand generations to offer a distinct survival advantage. The hunters who kept chasing sometimes brought home the meat that the less persistent ones could not. This mental surrogate for *optical* guidance could well have become the basis of the *cognitive* envisioning that characterized the emergence of human consciousness.

Top athletes often say that one of the keys to success in sport is "visualization"—imagining, as you practice, the performance you aspire to achieve when the real test comes. Coaches try to teach this technique, but in truth it's largely instinctive. I have watched young boys, who have no coach, playing basketball on a playground: "I'm Kobe! I look LeBron in the eye . . . I blow past him, I score!" When I was that age, before Kobe or LeBron or even Michael Jordan was born, I stood in my back yard in Westfield and declared, "I'm Billy Pierce, and I'm on the mound with a one-run lead against the Yankees! Whoever wins this game wins the pennant! Bases are loaded, bottom of the ninth! Mickey Mantle at bat! Two out, three balls, two strikes! I look at Lollar! He wants the curve! I shake it off! I'm going with my fast ball! Lollar is shaking his head, No! No! I wind up, I feel the power in my arm, I deliver, Mantle swings . . . HE'S OUT!"

It's not just kids who do this, but athletes at the highest level. John Parker recalled that Bill Rodgers, who won the New York Marathon and the Boston Marathon four times each, could still benefit by envisioning a runner who in sheer leg speed was even faster than he—such as Henry Rono, the Kenyan who in 1978 broke the world records for the 10,000 meters, 5,000 meters, and 3,000 meters. "I can remember doing interval workouts and thinking of Henry Rono's spectacular speed doing quarter miles or halves," Rodgers told Parker.[1]

At some point in a young athlete's growth, the fantasy may shift from imitating an already accomplished star to envisioning himself or herself as a star-to-be; it may move from an imaginary present to an anticipated future—from playing to planning. When this happens, the athlete is reenacting the experience of the persistence hunter. *Somewhere* out there becomes *sometime.* And eventually, *someday.* As a global society, we sometimes seem to have forgotten all about the *someday* that environmentalists called the "seventh generation," or simply "the human future." Maybe this is an area where our leaders really could learn from our athletes—not in showing how tough they are at "fighting" crime or terrorism or bloated government, but in how capable they are of envisioning the *real* threats we face and opportunities we may still have.

If the persistence hunter had an evolving ability to "see" around the bend in physical space, and therefore in time, then a critical part of looking ahead in time, and ultimately of successful envisioning and planning, is patience. *Impatience* meant trying to jump ahead to the end-game, when spotting the bend ahead was just the beginning. For the early hominid, to jump ahead would have required a technology he didn't have—a helicopter or Humvee—and he wasn't wired for the consequences of that jump. And *neither are we*, his descendants, even if we do have the technological means.

For us, jumping to the prey without engaging in the hunt meant missing a million critical signs on the trail. It meant building nuclear power plants without first finding long-term, earthquake-proof storage for radioactive waste that will remain deadly for centuries. It meant producing electricity without first grasping the impacts of the carbon dioxide emitted from coal-burning power plants. Coal wasn't just over-heating the planet; it was killing people directly. A few years after this 2001 race, the American Lung Association would report that emissions from coal-burning power plants were killing thirteen thousand Americans each year. And now I recalled that on that steep descent to Weverton, there were signs on the switchbacks—placed by the Forest Service—warning hikers not to take shortcuts because shortcutting triggers destructive erosion. On the scale of our civilization, we were ignoring or not noticing such signs. Our ability to build shortcut technologies had never given us sanction to destroy the terrain we were shortcutting.

I've discerned an intriguing irony in the capacities we have given ourselves to rush, take shortcuts, leap the bends—and miss the signs of what lies ahead. As our technological capabilities expand the powers of our legs with wheels or wings—or of our eyes with telescopes, our balance with gyroscopes, our arms with artillery, our ears with radio and TV, our memories with smartphones—the avalanche of poorly digested or undigested or contaminated data is blinding us to any integrated picture of our surroundings. The hunter-gatherer observed a thousand signs in every kilometer of the territory he was traversing, and to survive he had to know his role in it. We, overwhelmed with artificial distraction—spectator sports, celebrity, political posturing, gossip, scandal, soap operas, sitcoms, newscasts of the latest shootings and crashes, mindless text messages, and incessant deceptive advertising—are more and more *blinded* to what lies ahead.

For me, thanks to what I learned in my work with the environmental scientists and futurists, the signs of that blindness were staggering. The most memorable sign had come almost exactly nine years ago, on November 18, 1992, although it didn't hit me until several days later, when someone at my Worldwatch office gave me a copy of a press release. "A Threat to Human Survival," read the headline, and news editors around the world evidently must have rolled their eyes. The release had been issued by an organization called the Union of Concerned Scientists, under the title *World Scientists' Warning to Humanity*. For those who bothered to read it, the document stated: "We, the undersigned senior members of the world's scientific community, hereby warn all humanity of what lies ahead. A great change in the stewardship of the earth and life on it is required, if vast human misery is to be avoided and our global home on this planet is not to be irretrievably mutilated. . . . Humans and the natural world are on a collision course."[2]

The document described a deterioration of life systems that was rapidly worsening—as manifested by collapsing ocean fish populations, freshwater shortages in at least eighty countries, and the then-incipient prospect of global warming—a prospect that many of these scientists had already described as likely to raise sea level and bring city-obliterating mega storms in the coming decades. These trends, said the authors, "may so alter the living world that it will be unable to sustain life in the manner we know now."[3]

On the day this story was supposed to hit the front pages

of the Sunday papers and TV talk shows, I had been out for a long run on the wooded trails of Washington, DC's Rock Creek Park. Getting out for a two- or three-hour trail run was still my form of Sunday meditation and reflection, a respite from the tensions and turmoil of the work week. I had seen nothing about this report in the Sunday *Washington Post* when I sat down to read it after my run.

To busy news editors, the *World Scientists' Warning* might have looked, at a quick glance, like another of those periodic "The End Is Near" prophesies displayed from time to time by bearded old men with hand-lettered signs on street corners. But this statement was quite different: It was a carefully worded document signed by more than 1,575 of the world's leading biologists, chemists, physicists, ecologists, and earth scientists, including 101 Nobel Prize winners. Among its signers were the renowned astrophysicists Carl Sagan and Stephen Hawking; evolutionary biologists Stephen Jay Gould and Edward O. Wilson; population biologist Paul Ehrlich; economist Wassily Leontief; chemist Linus Pauling; DNA pioneer James Watson (co-discoverer of the double helix structure of DNA); and astronomer James Van Allen (for whom the earth's Van Allen Belt is named).

In its implications for the future of civilization, the *World Scientists' Warning* could well have been considered one of the most momentous manifestos ever presented to the public—on a par with Darwin's *Origin of Species*, or the American Declaration of Independence, or Martin Luther King Jr.'s "I Have a Dream" speech. Yet, it was ignored—or perhaps knowingly blacked out—by the major media. The day after the release, it seems not to have been reported in a single US newspaper. A front-page story in the *New York Times* that day recounted the struggle of a Muslim family to survive in war-torn Sarajevo. But the struggle of all humanity, present and future, to survive on an ecologically torn planet? The *Times* editors said they had not considered the story "newsworthy." The same curious response was offered by the *Washington Post*, the paper of record for every sort of crash. But the possibility that civilization itself might be headed for a crash?

That hadn't been an isolated moment of media amnesia, or misplaced press releases in busy news rooms. That same year, the first report of the world's top climate scientists from more than a hundred nations, the Intergovernmental Panel on Climate Change (IPCC), had been largely ignored or pushed to back pages as well. Then, in 1996, there was another momentous press release. This one, from the American Museum of Natural History in New York, announced the results of a national survey of scientists finding that a large majority of American biologists believed we were now in the midst of the largest mass extinction of species since the dinosaurs died out sixty-five million years ago—a staggering wake-up call to the increasingly threatened species *Homo sapiens*. That story, too, was largely ignored. The following year, when the United States was given an opportunity to provide global leadership in taking a small first step toward coping with the climate threat by endorsing the Kyoto Climate Treaty in 1997, the US Senate voted to oppose it, 95 to zero. If the mainstream media had given that treaty and what it meant just one-tenth of the coverage they'd given to the O. J. Simpson murder trial two years earlier, the ultimate effect might have been to save a hundred million lives in the years to come.

There were times when it seemed that quite possibly the most important single value of long-distance running for me was the reassurance it gave me that I do not have to be swept up by the systemic madness and myopia that seem to have seized control of my world. This towpath, out here past mile post 83, still had a little wildness, which allowed me to stay connected to a little of my own wildness. I was able at least to keep my balance, at a time when the civilized world seemed to have been blindfolded by thieves and sent speeding toward a wreck.

For all its loneliness, part of what had given this footpath such a hold on my heart, even now as my legs grew weak, was that no motor vehicles were allowed on it. When I reached the road in a few minutes, there would be cars. But now, as the dam appeared suddenly, far upriver to the left—a little less imposing than I had imagined, the brushstroke a little less impressionistic and more hard-edged—I felt a relief and an uplift. The envisioned goal had finally become an optically visible one—the mental surrogate transformed to a physical reality, and I felt a needed sense of reconnection with what I was hoping to do.

13

COUNTRY ROAD

The Blessing and Curse of
Competition: Why Vince Lombardi
Was Dead Wrong

JUST BEFORE THE dam, the course took a hard right off the towpath onto a narrow country road. As I hit the pavement, I could feel my competitiveness intensifying, the low-fuel warning light in my head notwithstanding. Maybe I was a little too much like one of those supply-side zealots who want to "drill, drill, drill!" despite the warnings of both petroleum geologists and climate scientists that we are nearing the economic and ecological limits of oil consumption. It may have been partly because the remaining distance in the race— eight miles once you get to the top of the hill up from the dam—was now in the same range as most of the road races we ran in the 1960s and '70s, when the Road Runners Club of America was taking hold. So, eight miles now felt like, *OK, it's race time.* And partly, the feeling was triggered by going onto pavement, which is faster than dirt or gravel. My feet and legs had a lingering muscle-memory of how fast I can go on asphalt if I really get into the zone. The fastest ultra I had ever run was that one in New York City a quarter-century ago, in which I had captured the moment of the final two hundred yards forever, on the slightly rolling paved loop road through Central Park. This rural Maryland road, if you replaced the buildings around Central Park with open fields (would those apartment and hotel owners mind?), was a little like that.

Just a couple of minutes up the road, though, I heard footsteps from behind and another Marine went past me, fast. I hadn't seen him when I looked back at the dam turnoff, and he must have hit that climb at the start of the road like it was San Juan Hill. It was Tom Hethcoat, one of the guys from Quantico. There were at least fourteen men from the two Marines teams in the race, but, except for the one who'd politely informed me that I was bleeding, I hadn't seen any of them in the past four hours. Most of them had to be far ahead of me, because they'd gone racing up that first hill from Boonsboro six hours ago, and I hadn't seen hide or hair of them since. On the other hand, in an ultra you can sometimes pass people at an aid station—or be passed—and not realize it because you're focused on getting your bottle refilled. Or, you can pass people but be so in the zone that you don't notice who they are. I had expected to reel in some of those guys eventually, but . . . instead, here was Tom Hethcoat pulling away from me.

At the same time, I felt a little spunk coming back into me. I grew up in a country where competitiveness is a virtue right up there with godliness. There were countless Horatio Alger–like stories about the kid who didn't have quite the physical gifts of some other kids, but who became a star because he had such a "fire in his belly." CEOs love sales or marketing executives who have that fire; it's how sports heroes become the models for the free-market economy. And on one level, I love it too; I love to race against other guys.

But on another level, I know that competitiveness takes a heavy toll. What it takes to be a serious competitor consumes a staggering amount of time and energy—a lot of your life. And you don't really have any choice in the matter; it's compulsory, even if the compulsion comes from inside your own body and brain. I couldn't decide *not* to train and race hard. Clarence DeMar once commented, "Most fans think that I'm as tied up with running as a smoker is with his weed or a drinker with his liquor, and that for me to quit would cause nervous and physical disaster. Unless I lose a leg, become bedridden or go to jail, I never intend to find out whether this is right."[1]

At forty-two miles, with just a little over an hour to go, was this any time to be feeling ambivalence about competition? Experienced athletes and coaches all know that emotional hesitancy is an invitation to failure. And military officers know that it can be fatal. And maybe that's a valid observation for twenty-year-old athletes or soldiers. But for a sixty-year-old man balancing the emotional pulls of family, country, and world, as well as the management of his own body and soul, ambivalence goes with the territory. I knew that even as a youth I'd probably have been a disaster as a soldier because I'd have asked too many questions and wanted to discuss the societal ramifications of too many of the orders I was given. As an older man, I was chronically in danger of being a disaster on every front I cared about. Here I was, closing in on the biggest goal of my life, daring to question what it really meant.

When our little Elizabeth was eight or nine, she played on a junior soccer team one summer, and when the girls lost five or six straight games and started feeling like losers, and then their coach quit because he said they weren't winners, it broke my heart. Maybe that kind of reaction, shared by others, helped account for the now popular practice, by road and trail race organizers, of saying that in a running race, *everyone is a winner*. Yet, that didn't feel quite right to me either. Giving a medal to everyone who ran a race, as was now common practice, seemed to me to devalue the symbol. In the 1950s and '60s, medals had generally been awarded in running events only at championships, and only three medals were awarded for each event. The first time I won a medal, in my junior year of high school, it was an indescribable thrill—and now I still had that medal in a cabinet, even though almost everything else from high school, including my diploma, had long since been lost. Today and tonight, everyone who finished the JFK would get a medal, and it would be a *big* mother, five times the size of that little bronze memento of a forgotten high school mile, but it just wouldn't be the same.

The difference between getting that third medal and finishing "out of the running" in fourth could be gut-wrenching. There'd been that memorable time when I'd gotten the third place medal at the national 50-Mile in 1976. And I vividly recalled what happened to Don Kardong, one of the great marathoners of the time, that same year. Don had experienced *both* sides of that excruciating third-versus-fourth place divide, in the most epic way one could imagine. First was the US Olympic marathon trial for the 1976 games. The trials race was staged in America's distance-running mecca, Eugene, Oregon, and forty-nine men who had qualified for the trial were entered. By the last few miles, four were still in contention. Frank Shorter and Bill Rodgers were out in front, matching stride for stride. Don Kardong and Tony Sandoval, who happened to be close friends, were running stride for stride in the race for third. It seemed clear by now that Shorter and Rodgers had a lock on the first two places, which meant one of the two friends running third and fourth would make the team and the other would not. There was probably nothing that either of these guys could want more for his friend than to see him make the Olympic team—and nothing more that he could want for himself. I can only imagine what a remote MRI of Don Kardong's brain would have displayed as he realized that he was the stronger of the two that day and was going to leave his friend behind and go get that third place. What that scan would have registered—the storm of simultaneous realization, ambivalence, thrill, regret, *and* unhesitating resolve— might have blown the circuits in the machine! Don made the Olympic team. His friend went home. And yet, fate was not finished with Don. In the Montreal Olympics, he went on to run the race of his life—and finished fourth. I don't think even God had a laugh that day. That was also the day that the iconic runner Steve Prefontaine, whose dreams of Olympic gold in Munich had been upset by the tragedy of the Israeli athlete massacre, and whose disappointment there had been transformed into an even more compelling resolve to win the 10,000 meters in Montreal, was conspicuously absent from that city—having died in a car accident.

My awe at Don Kardong's epic battles for the bronze might seem inconsistent with my distress at seeing a group of young girls feeling like losers. I don't claim to be consistent. But I also see a significant difference between a competition that always ends with a binary win-or-lose outcome, and one that offers many degrees of success. A fourth-place finish in the Olympic marathon is bittersweet at worst, and in most eyes it is a tremendous success. Maybe my problem is not that I'm inconsistent about competitiveness, but that I really am ambivalent. Competition, like technology—to paraphrase that long-ago mission statement from the scientists at IR&T—can enrich our life or poison it; it can bring great feelings of achievement, but can also make young girls feel like dorks.

I should mention that after the sore-loser coach of Elizabeth's soccer team quit, a couple of the players' fathers stepped in, and the girls began winning and went all the way to the league's championship game. They lost that last game but went home with great feelings of achievement. In the end, it wasn't winning that had been necessary for success, but the satisfaction of having survived and bounced back from a thoughtless put-down.

We Americans have been exposed to an almost-never-challenged doctrine of competition as the key to success in all things. Whether it's in school, business, sport, or the pursuit of national supremacy, we're taught that the goal is to win. I wondered how many times I'd heard a political or business leader quote football coach Vince Lombardi's revered doctrine, "winning isn't everything . . . it's the *only* thing." I'd never heard anyone challenge that, except maybe the parents of Joan Benoit, who recalled in her book *Running Tide* that, when she was a young girl, her parents did *not want* their children to be consumed by competitiveness: "Winning was neither everything nor the only thing. It was one of many things," Joan wrote of her parents' perspective. "None of us viewed life through a tunnel formed by a single, all-consuming passion."[2] Diversity of interests in her early development must have served Joan well. Evidently in accord with the elder Benoits, I think Lombardi was mistaken. What troubled me was that if the only goal is to win, it is also to make other people lose. But for most runners, I doubt that "winning" or "losing" is even relevant. That may be why that question "Did you win?" can be so disconcerting. Most of the participants in a road or trail race do not expect to either win *or* lose. Some runners and coaches have gotten around the win-lose problem by suggesting that what you're doing in a footrace is "competing with yourself." I don't like that phrase, which sounds slightly schizophrenic, but for thousands of runners, I think it's closer to what's really happening, because one of the legacies of our evolution has been internal tugs-of-war between different drives. Back in the days when troubled people who could afford it went to see psychoanalysts, it was said that our ids, egos, and superegos were all competing for control of our behavior. Psychoanalysis has since been left in the dustbin of obsolescent science, but evolutionary biologists and neuroscientists have confirmed that different parts of the brain developed at different stages of our evolution and sometimes really do have conflicting holds on us. Traits that were valuable at an earlier time (such as accumulating fat to get through the winter, for example) don't serve the same function now and can cause a lot of trouble.

In popular media and culture (the sports news, business news, cooking shows, *American Idol*, college admissions, presidential politics, spelling bees, the Oscars), competitiveness is uncritically regarded as a virtue, and especially an American virtue. For a lot of conservatives, it's an ideology. For economists, it's a virtual religion. If you are *insanely* competitive, rather than be urged to seek counseling, you will be admired and sought out—by coaches, political strategists, and executive search committees.

When the embrace of competitiveness is that absolute, though, I think a little ambivalence is actually healthier—and may, paradoxically, provide a competitive advantage! The secret is that 95 percent of what happens in the competition was already determined by the time you went to the starting line— some of it over years, some over the last eight months. And how successfully you lay the groundwork for that 95 percent depends very much on your mental and emotional flexibility. If you're so fanatical that you can never take a day off—say, when you're grieving a loss, or job searching, or sick—you're not likely to even *last* through the years. And if you're so rigidly adherent to a particular method of training that you're not open to fresh ideas, you're not only at the top of your learning curve but probably over the hill. A big test of how well you can do at age sixty depends on how well you can keep experimenting and discovering as if you were sixteen.

By the time of the 2001 JFK, I firmly believed that living with ambivalence—often feeling torn, and always asking new questions—is, in fact, an essential part of being an enduring individual or society. It begins with how we evolved. Our Paleolithic ancestors, to survive in a hot African or Asian environment, had to develop a cardiovascular system that could enable them to go long distances in the heat while meeting competing demands on the available blood supply within their own bodies. The muscles needed the blood to stay fueled and oxygenated for as long as it took to run a wild horse to exhaustion, which could be hours. But because the sun was radiating heat and the body was generating even more heat by metabolizing the meat of the last horse the hunting party had killed, some of the same blood supply serving the muscles was also being called on to carry excess heat to the skin, to be dumped off into the air. It was a routine internal tug-of-war, like the tension between a man sitting on a couch during the football post-season with beer cans and empty chip bags piled up around him, and his wife or girlfriend asking him in the middle of a critical fourth-quarter drive to please take out the trash. Can you watch a touchdown and take out the trash at the same time? The Paleolithic runner *could* hunt and get rid of waste at the same time.

An orange signboard on the shoulder of the road ahead indicated five miles to go in the race. It was past two o'clock, at this time of year only a little over two hours before it would start to get dark, and it felt like the temperature had dropped several degrees since I left the towpath. I felt a chill but reminded myself that I was lucky it wasn't hot. I recalled the time when, as a spring chicken of forty-nine, I ran the Badwater 137—a 137-mile midsummer race across Death Valley and up Mt. Whitney. The rules required that each runner have a support vehicle, which was prohibited from moving along with the runner, but could leapfrog every three miles or so and stop for the crew to provide ice water or sustenance as the runner went by. In those days, I still hadn't quite figured out how to fuel for an ultra. I really don't know what I was thinking, but at one of the stops I decided to eat a slice of bread. When I reached the crew again three miles later, I still had almost the entire slice uneaten in my hand, and it had turned to toast.

Yet, in a whole day of running steadily across a desert in temperatures over 120 degrees and no shade, miraculously *I* didn't turn to toast. The human body, if properly cared for, is astonishingly proficient at maintaining ecological balances—between fueling and waste, between oxygen delivery to the muscles and heat-transfer to the skin, or between resting very tired legs and remaining upright. At least I knew that homeostasis—the maintaining of balances between competing physiological demands—is basic to optimal performance, whether you're asleep, watching TV, running slowly across a desert, or heading for the finish of a fifty-mile race. Whether it's the work of the blood, hormones, left and right brains, or new and old neural pathways, competing demands are a part of us from birth to death.

Socially, as well, those tugs-of-war and the resulting sense of being conflicted, or ambivalent, are a part of our inherited nature. The Darwinian proclivity of the human male to disseminate his genes competes with the female's instinct to hold a mate who is committed to bringing home food and protecting the family. Archetypal tensions, between male and female, young and old, individual and community, play out in the never-ending dynamics of society at large.

How well a society manages its inherently competing forces is a major determinant of how successfully—or how long—it will endure. If competing factions take inflexible positions, the result can be pervasive dysfunction or war. I thought of Paul Shepard's theory about the frustrated instinct to hunt and its transmogrification into the hunting down of other men. In the history of civilization, as Jared Diamond and others have argued, the most inflexible position humanity ever took was its adoption of domestication and consequent abandonment of the wild. It was not just animals and plants that were domesticated and tamed, but ourselves. I recalled a comment the Spanish philosopher José Ortega y Gasset made: that because hunting is a "deep and permanent yearning in the human condition," there is a chronic fury in all people to whom it is denied.[3] To run well—and replay that hunt—is to quell that fury.

And more to the point, in these last few miles, to quell the fury would be to run well. I needed, again, to slow the turbulence.

I was old enough to know that there are very few ways that an older athlete can compete on even terms, not to say advantageous terms, with a younger one. In a sprint or a leap or other anaerobic feat, there are none. And in an endurance event, *almost* none. There are two ways, though, that it can sometimes happen. First, the older runner can take advantage of having had more opportunity to review the evolutionary and cultural history of our kind, and thereby to recognize what the competing impulses within us are, and how to manage them for optimal results. As I pulled even with another runner, who as of that moment had run forty-six miles in exactly the same time as I had, I thought that what could make the small difference that decides our competition in the end is my ability to look at this younger runner—whom I didn't know, but now had a uniquely shared experience with—not as an adversary but as a companion in adventure. It seemed counterintuitive, but what my experience told me was that in its impact on blood chemistry, it could be the difference. Adrenaline would not be helpful now.

Possibly more important was that, while most of the miles I had run in my life had been solitary, some of the most enjoyable and memorable times had been training runs with companions: the kids I'd coached at the George School, teammates at Swarthmore, and my DC neighbor Bob Harper, the guy who first told me about the JFK. Bob and I had even done a practice run on the AT from South Mountain to Weverton once, and—sure enough—I had fallen on the rocks! But particularly significant, from this standpoint, were my runs with a fellow Swarthmore alum, Bob Zoellick, who was a grad student in Washington when I was working with Ted Taylor at IR&T. Bob Z. and I had a little rivalry going with our respective marathon times, and sometimes ran workouts together in Rock Creek Park in the early evening. Years later, I would realize that Bob and I were political adversaries (he'd been appointed president of the World Bank, while I published commentaries sharply critical of the World Bank's impacts on the global environment), and that if we had talked politics as we ran, we'd have clashed. But instead we just ran, leaping over fallen logs and enjoying the cooling air of the early evening, and whatever tensions our respective work days brought were dispelled.

The second advantage I felt an older runner might have—perhaps counter to conventional young/old stereotypes— was his greater experience in adapting to change, especially given a world that had changed much more rapidly than in any earlier era. I was born two months before Pearl Harbor and lived through World War II, the Korean War, the Vietnam War, the Cold War, the Kosovo War, Desert Storm, the Rwanda Genocide, and now Afghanistan, and what would be next? More wars and more bitter divisions would follow, of course. And being able to roll with the punches, the way Muhammad Ali did, was an on-the-run skill, both physical and psychological.

For example, we were now past the part of the road that had been closed off by the police. Orange cones marked off a couple of feet of pavement for the runners, but cars were passing with increasing frequency as we came to the outskirts of the town. A lot of the cars slowed as they passed, and their occupants called out words of encouragement ("Good job! Good job! Not far, now!"), which gave me a big kick. Would a younger runner get the same lift from hearing such friendly voices from cars? Maybe a little, but I suspected that a lot of it would go under a younger person's radar. People in cars are rarely hostile to runners these days, since runners are now everywhere and are part of the background drivers pass—as are cars for runners. For someone who'd been running as long as I had, though, that hadn't always been the case. In the 1960s, a guy running along the side of the road was an unusual sight, and it often seemed to trigger provocative comments from male drivers and their passengers. Once, a half-full can of beer flew out of a passenger's window and splatted on the pavement at my feet. Other times, cars swerved close enough to drive me off the road. More than once (before the days of bright, techie apparel, when we wore grey or white cotton gym shorts), I heard the taunt, "What are you running in your underwear for?" followed by raucous laughter. But by now, that hadn't happened in many years, and friendly reactions from cars actually made me grin, even if my face was tired. It was another small thing (like not regarding other runners as adversaries and not regarding fatigue as an enemy), but small things—especially in the final miles of a race where 95 percent of what you accomplish was determined before the day began—do make a difference. When you're sixty and not sixteen, you need to be not only tough, but savvy in perhaps unexpected ways.

There had been times in the past year when the running made me as high as it did when I *was* 16, just as I suppose there are times when an alcoholic or compulsive gambler or hedge-fund manager feels like the king of the world. But most of the time, now, the burden seemed heavier. I couldn't tolerate cold as I once had, and on a dreary winter day I could experience quite an internal conflict—one part of me wanting to get out and hit the trail in training for the next race, the other wanting to curl up with a blanket and a good book. Sometimes the trail won, sometimes the book. I knew that if I hadn't been addicted enough to get out for at least a good many of those gray days, I wouldn't be in touch with the genetic messages I was receiving from my hunter-gatherer ancestors—about what terrible ordeals they and *their* ancestors endured, and how the singular strengths they developed to compensate for their mammalian shortcomings enabled modern humans to have the adaptive capabilities we now have. We, the builders of civilization, would not have had the endurance, patience, and ability to envision a thing that still lies out of sight ahead of us (the house, the temple, the city . . . and then the atomic bomb, the moon landing, the Internet, the symphony orchestra) if we didn't continue to practice these arts.

Sport can be exhausting, painful, and disappointing, but at least it doesn't leave us raped or dead, like the losers in a resource war. It allows us to compete with others without maiming or murdering them. And if I was still wondering why millions of people who don't seem as compulsively competitive as I am nonetheless run races, a conversation I had one day with my cousin-in-law David Meggyesy may offer an answer. David played linebacker for the St. Louis Cardinals (now Arizona Cardinals) of the National Football League, but quit at the peak of his career to write the book *Out of Their League*, exposing the corruption and abuses of college and pro football. He also got involved with a movement to expose the abuses of cutthroat capitalist competition. As a highly competitive pro athlete himself, he had credibility about this subject in a way that some of us amateurs can't claim to. In his book, so devastating was his criticism that some readers could have made the mistake of thinking he was a disillusioned former player with a grudge. But in fact, David loved playing football and enjoyed knocking ball-carriers off their feet, and in a letter to me he explained the seeming paradox of players beating each other up on the field *and* being good friends with each other:

> We realize we are playing this game together and fundamentally need each other. No opponent, no game. Interestingly, the roots of "competition" are *com*, which means "with" or "together," and *petere*, "to strive."[4]

This isn't a thought that just leaps to mind in every football player, I suspect. It's a benefit of training—a different kind of training than Vince Lombardi ever directed. David explained that the kind of strength that enables men to strive together takes a kind of training of the spirit, just as much as blocking or tackling strength takes training of the body. I was passing the three-mile orange sign now and felt like I'd been training my spirit for these last three miles for the past three decades.

14

WILLIAMSPORT

If You Fall, Then You Crawl.
What Is It About Finishing?

IT WAS A tough-love reminder of my vulnerability as an aging, half-naked human hoping to survive on a formidable planet, that in these last few miles even a small hill felt like a mountain. Was God grinning? Were the Native Americans right about there being a trickster out there? When I saw the big orange "3" halfway up another small hill, though, I was as hooked as a starving wolf chasing a fat rabbit off the rim of a cliff. I've always felt that once I get inside three miles, I can finish no matter what. Passing the sign, for a moment, I actually felt a flicker of strength.

Still, I was wary of the trickster. And in the world of empirical science, where I'd been hanging out for so many years, nothing is ever certain. I recalled one time when I was running the Boston Marathon—not one of my better years there—and made it over Heartbreak Hill, then hit the wall. The glycogen was gone, which is quite a helpless feeling. Reduced to burning fat, long before I'd ever heard of the carbohydrate fire, I entered the purgatory of that dream where you're being chased by something awful and you can only move in slow motion.

Hitting the wall was a rare experience for me in those days, but when it happened I had a simple strategy for getting through. For me, as for most runners, finishing was the thing. No matter what, I had to finish. My strategy was to take note of the remaining distance, then begin running a quarter-mile at a time, counting down. In an exhausted condition, it's easier to contemplate distances in yards than in miles. Just 440 yards at a time. Imagine one lap on my old high school track. Then do it again. With each hard-earned quarter-mile, there's a little reward: another quarter-mile in the bag.

Boston by now was a huge tunnel of spectators, cheering and shouting to us passing strangers: "Go number 512!" "Go Jill's Dad!" (reading the hand-lettered sign on a man's jersey). I jogged to the side of the road and asked the sea of faces, "How far to the finish?"

"Three miles!" called out a man.

"Thanks." I spotted a building I guessed was a quarter-mile down the road and began my countdown: two and three-quarters to go, then run for a while. Then two and a half, and run for a while. Then two and a quarter . . . and so on, and on.

When I'd worked it down to what I figured was just a mile to go, I was utterly exhausted but knew that, come hell or high water, I could drag myself *one* more mile. Just to confirm my situation, I called out to the crowd, "How far, now?"

"Three miles! You're almost there!"

I have no doubt that both of my cheery informants meant well. But as I've learned over the years since then, people who live in a country where most mobility is automotive often have a very poor sense of distance and sometimes don't really know where they are.

Another time, in a high-altitude trail race years later, I experienced a *Groundhog Day*–like repeat of that trickster encounter, but this time with both estimates of the remaining distance offered by aid-station volunteers who'd been carried to their posts over circuitous jeep roads. And this time, the second response, by a worker who was eager to be helpful but apparently not sure which side of the mountain he was on, actually *increased* the estimated remaining distance by half a mile. By then, though, I was older and wiser. I knew how much God might enjoy having one more good laugh before the day was done.

I had also learned, by that time, of a study of human mental mapping that had serious implications for a society in which new technologies were supplanting more and more of what people once did with their own physical *or* mental faculties. It wasn't just SUVs supplanting hiking shoes; it was the GPS in the SUV taking over for your brain. Researchers at McGill University in Canada and the University of London in the UK scanned the brains of hundreds of taxi drivers in London and found that drivers who had relied on GPS devices to find their way around the city for three years or longer had diminished capacity in the hippocampus, the part of the brain that plays a central role in our ability to remember and find our way. In fact, compared with drivers who had relied on their own abilities, the hippocampuses in the GPS group had actually *shrunk*. A muscle that isn't used will atrophy, and evidently that can happen with brain functions as well.

■　■　■

We humans are such *goofies*, as the anthropologist Paul Shepard would put it. *Goofies* is his word for an animal that has the genes of wild ancestors but has been captured and excessively domesticated—compelled to live in the highly artificial world of civilization. When we modern humans run a race, we run wild for a few hours, but then the run approaches its end. It's like approaching the end of a wondrous dream and waking up with a powerful yearning. For what?

That yearning begins long before the race begins, in the daydreaming about running a marathon or ultra. It builds intensity in the fantasizing you do over the months of training and comes to a head as you run the race itself and approach its finish. What began months or years ago as a fantasy escalates into a powerful homing instinct, an almost unstoppable volition to *reach completion*. Over the years, I'd seen some amazing outcomes of that volition, in which we actually experience the wild hunters that we are. It happened at all long distances, from 5K high school cross-country races to hundred-milers and beyond. The drive to *finish* the race has become so primal and powerful that it defies logic.

There was the time a man named Bob Bohnke, of Salisbury, Maryland, was running in a half-marathon. Maybe the race director had promised the town officials that the runners would stay on the shoulder. In any case, Bohnke was running on the pavement, half a mile from the finish, when he noticed three police cars parked just ahead. As he approached, an officer ordered him to "get off the road and onto the shoulder, or stand to be arrested!" Bohnke replied, "You can't be serious!"—and continued running on the edge of the pavement. One of the cops shouted another warning, and Bohnke's response later raised a question as to whether maybe he'd been "bohnked" on his head as a child.

"Catch me!" he shouted back.

"You're under arrest!" shouted the three policemen in unison.

Even then, Bob Bohnke was not to be deterred. He ran a

hard 800 yards, perhaps imagining that he could outrun a bullet, and he *finished*. And *then* he was arrested.

Then there was the case of Dennis Rainear, who did *not* outrun a bullet—he stopped one cold, but still finished. In 1978, Rainear was in the tenth mile of the Grand Valley Marathon in Colorado when he was shot in the head by a hunter. As reported in *Running Times*, he kept right on running, completing the last sixteen miles with a .22 caliber slug in his head. The magazine published a photo of the x-ray, showing a bullet stuck in Rainear's skull like a small carrot in a snowman.

One of the most memorable finishes I've ever heard of was that of Geoff Smith in the 1983 New York City Marathon. Smith ran his heart out, leading the race coming into Central Park, but struggling mightily to hang on, with the great New Zealand Olympian Rod Dixon closing in. Marathon runners sometimes joke that "the twenty-six miles isn't so bad, it's the last 385 yards that get you." On this day, that was literally true. For a marathoner, Rod Dixon had exceptional leg speed; he'd won the bronze medal in the Olympic 1,500 meters in Munich. It came down to a dead sprint, and ten yards from the finish, Geoff Smith—after leading one of the world's greatest footraces for twenty-six miles, 375 yards— tripped and fell. "Dixon was photographed leaping into the air and then kneeling on the pavement in theatrical ecstasy. The photos appeared on magazine covers, and one was nominated for a Pulitzer prize," we reported.[1] In the photos, Smith is off to the side in a very awkward sprawl. But never mind, he got to his feet and *finished*.

In the years since then, I've come to realize that apparently because we humans will do anything in our power to capture that moment yearned for, *many* runners have fallen in the final yards of a race—and then, if necessary, *crawled* across the line. Some of the most heroic of these, maybe because when we are young we are still at our wildest, have been in high school cross-country meets.

In California, for example, I would later hear about a young woman named Holland Reynolds, who on the day of this JFK was only seven years old, but who nine years later would be good enough to lead her University High School in San Francisco to a California state championship. On the day of the big meet, she was running in second place, nearing the finish and giving it her all, when she was overcome with what appeared to be heat exhaustion and collapsed. Unable to stand up, she crawled the last ten feet to the finish. It was good enough to win the team title, and her happy teammates crowded into the ambulance with her to celebrate.

In the Massachusetts state championship, Ben Perron of St. John's High School in Southboro, similarly giving it his all, fell to the ground sixty yards from the finish, got up, and tried continuing but fell over again, backward. He got up again, fell backward again. He finally crawled on all fours to within a yard of the finish, at which point even crawling didn't work, so he made himself *roll* over the line.

In the Louisiana state championship, Christian Bergeron of St. Paul's School in Covington was running in thirteenth place when he went down twenty-five yards from the finish, got up and fell again repeatedly, including twice over backward, but finally dragged himself over the line on hands and knees. He lost twenty-five places in twenty-five yards, but he *finished.*

And then there was the Ohio state championship, where Claire Markwardt of Berkshire High School was running surprisingly well, considering that she was recovering from a stress fracture in her left leg. When she was just four hundred yards from the finish, however, she heard and felt a sharp crack in that leg. She would later learn that her tibia had snapped. She never thought of stopping, though. At forty-five yards out, she felt another snap and went down hard—this time with her fibula broken in half. She, too, crawled to the finish, with a time of 20:24:07, only eighteen seconds off her personal best.

■ ■ ■

So, what is it about *finishing*? If you run a marathon and complete the twenty-six miles, 385 yards, you'll be memorably satisfied. But if you run a fifty-mile race and have to quit at forty-nine miles, you'll be deeply disappointed. The distance is arbitrary, but the need to *finish*—whatever the designated distance—is like the need to eat. Where did we get this? A short answer might be that it comes *from* the need to eat. More broadly, I sense that it relates to the way we became neurologically organized by our experience of hunger, thirst, and sexual desire, all of which can etch intensely vivid and memorable moments at the point of satisfaction. But I'm also guessing that it has to do with a genetic memory of the end of the long hunt that helped *enable* those other satisfactions.

For early human hunters, the killing of a larger, faster, stronger animal must have had enormous significance—not only for the tribe's survival but for the hunter's evolving sense of individual identity. When it came to going after a dangerous mammoth, the humans almost certainly had to hunt in a pack.

Implicit in the cooperation between the hunter distracting the quarry and his companion rushing in with the rock or spear was an understanding that the long pursuit they had made was *not* just a mindless rush to see which man could make the fatal thrust and claim all the meat. Some hunters would play supporting roles in exchange for a share of the prize secured by others. That kind of cooperation required being able to envision beyond the kill, to the return to the hearth—to the communal devouring. And if the hunters could look ahead in time, it is likely that they could also look back. At the hearth, the memory of the hunt lingered and, as language developed, was eventually shared just as was the food itself. Recalling which of the individual hunters had actually made the kill would have had a selective benefit, as it helped organize the division of labor for a successful hunt next time. For everyone to simply swarm over the quarry each time like crows over roadkill would have invited an early demise for all. For market-share monopolists and cutthroat competitors: a thing to consider.

So, knowing which hunter had a strong arm, a lethal technique with a rock or spear, or a sense of how the quarry would likely behave had a survival value. Natural selection favored not only the hunters who could make the kill but also those who could recognize the spear-thrower and give him logistic support, which he very much needed to have. If you knew how to provide that support—to skillfully track spoor before the chase begins or help carry the prize back to the cave after the kill—you may have had as much chance of providing meat to your children and mate as the spear-thrower did. Upper-body strength was an essential complement to enduring legs and lungs. The prize-bearers were part of the spear-thrower's triumph, so his thrill was also theirs. We have inherited that sharing of the kill in such familiar phenomena as the spontaneous exultation of all eleven members of a soccer team when one of them kicks the winning goal. For consciousness to grow, a sense of personal identity—and of your most realistic hopes and best strategies for realizing those hopes—also had to grow. Just as significantly, your sense of the identities of others, and your relationships with them, had to grow.

It may seem bizarre, to anyone who knows me, to hear me

suggest that the experience of killing fellow mammals (or being part of a band that did) was a defining experience in the evolution of human consciousness. I'm not only an old Quaker peacenik, but a vegetarian! But I also could not deny what all the evidence I could marshal was telling me: that our species had advanced by learning to hunt over large territories—the kinds of territories Lawrence of Arabia's nomad fighters would cover. We didn't have the teeth, claws, and backhoe jaws of our prey, but somehow we ate *them* before they could eat *us*. Our ancestors' campsites are littered with the bones of the animals they killed—whether for food, fur, horn, bone, hide, hormones, or in self-defense. What was less clear was what role the hunt had played in the development of our ancestors' awareness. And the murkiness of that question seemed to be made even murkier by the realization that even today, a lot of people are *not* very aware.

■ ■ ■

When I read the accounts of Paul Shepard, Bernd Heinrich, and others who have pondered the origins of human consciousness, here's what comes through most clearly: While the moment of the kill may have lived large in the hominid's evolving memory, it was only the relatively brief climax to a very long day of quiet tracking. Contrary to our twenty-first century notion of the good life being a procession of titillating climaxes, one after another (how cool is a high-scoring football game, with touchdown after touchdown!), our prehistory had to have been one of long treks, patient observation, and gradually developing mental vision. The climax of the hunt was the culmination of a huge amount of intervening experience. That might explain why the kill loomed so large in myth. It was not just a critical moment for the survival of the tribe; it was also, sometimes, the end of a long journey and the inspiration for a new journey that would require new faith and, again, patience.

The intervening experience was not just the scouting and tracking of the hunt itself. Our ape ancestors did not just step out of the forest and go forth in search of a mammoth. The transition took tens of thousands and perhaps even hundreds of thousands of years, and before we killed anything big we probably spent a long time watching other, more experienced, animals kill. Perhaps for many millennia we ate leftovers after lions ate the prime cuts, but waiting for the lion to leave his dinner may have been another key part of the early development of our observational and anticipatory powers.

Before that long period of flirtation with the lion's domain, where we were on the verge of trying our own hand at the big kill, there may have been an even longer period of more mundane food-gathering, hunting smaller animals, gathering worms or snails, collecting berries and tubers and seeds. And those skills, too, we still bring into the world hardwired into us. When I was a kid, I went through two periods of Indian-like hunting and stalking that I didn't learn from anyone. Around age ten, I became fascinated with reptiles and spent long summer afternoons trying to find them. When I caught a turtle or garter snake, it was a great thrill. I didn't want to kill it, though; I just wanted to catch it.

Often, I crouched at the bank of a pond watching for a species called the Eastern painted turtle (so named for the yellow and red markings around the rim of its bottom shell, or plastron—somehow, as a ten-year-old, I knew what a "plastron" was, as well as what a "carapace" was). I learned that I could spot a turtle by just the small black tip of its nose above the pond's surface. A water turtle has to come up for air, even when it's being stalked, but evolution has given it excellent camouflage; when it floats in a murky pond with only its nose poking up, all you can see from above the pond is what looks like the end of a waterlogged stick. But I could tell the difference, even if the water was too muddy or the reflection of the sky too bright on the surface to reveal anything submerged. One time, in a moment of preadolescent impulsiveness that might well have won me a Darwin Award (given to those who have contributed to the future of humanity by doing something stupid enough to remove them from the gene pool before they can reproduce), I saw a turtle's nose and dove into the water having no idea what invisible tree stumps or rocks might await me, but guessing well enough where the turtle would dive. The thrill of catching it was exquisite. Submerged tree stump-wise, I lucked out.

Maybe I lucked out in another way, as well. I grew up just a few years before TV got its clutches on kids. My family didn't own a TV, and my boyhood pursuits around the woods and ponds may have allowed me to become more attuned to my inner hunter and to the slow pace of life in the natural world than would be the experience of kids a few years later. For the children of the mid-1950s and later, the innate patience of the persistence hunter may have been overridden and buried by the high-suspense, quick-draw gunfights of TV Westerns and the even more high-speed dramas that would follow.

I was far from alone in this sort of sublimation. Decades later, around the area where we lived in Manassas, Virginia, I'd often see men prowling construction sites with metal detectors, looking for Civil War relics—bullets, belt buckles, buttons. These people were not amateur archeologists or anthropologists any more than I was an amateur herpetologist or mineralogist. It's the *discovery* they wanted, I'm pretty sure. I see signs that this is a widespread kind of urge among humans.

In reading the accounts of paleoanthropologists, we can easily oversimplify the lives of early humans, because the artifacts that survive now are relatively few—the ones that survive millennia of organic decay, or at least can be carbon-dated. There may have been many hundreds of varieties of flora and fauna that our ancestors knew and sought for purposes we know nothing about—and most traces of which have disappeared. The excitement they evoked when found would have been reinforced by evolution, because the more exciting it was, the longer you'd persist in the search and the more likely you'd find what was needed to cure an illness or meet a nutritional need. There's not much trace of that thrill in the remains dug up by paleontologists, unless it's in the rare fragment of glacier-frozen DNA or in the paintings of running animals found on cave walls. But there's more than a trace in the living descendants of those early humans—in *us*.

■　■　■

Whether it's in the endurance of a single individual or the sustainability of a whole society, the real story is not the quick excitements, like the dramatic last few yards of a race, but the long and quiet endeavor that leads up to it. Of course, with our short-circuited attention spans and addiction to climactic moments, we love dramatic finishes. They're what our media watch for on those rare occasions when they actually cover a running event. I admire a gutsy finish as much as anyone, without reservation. For me, those kids who crawled across the finish line rank right up there with the last-second touchdown runs that have won Super Bowls. But those kids never would have qualified for their respective state championships to begin with, without many hours of training they did over the preceding months. And then there was that hard three miles they all ran before they fell. If 95 percent of the runner's success is achieved before he or she even goes to the starting line, then 99.9 percent is done before the finish line is even within sight. A dramatic finish excites us because it evokes the primordial thrill of the kill and takes only a minute, but it tells us nothing of the long journey—the months of training and then the full length of the race itself—that preceded it.

What is lost in our perception of sustained endurance activity is the huge role that that quiet activity (as distinguished from the actual pursuit of prey) played in the development of awareness. The long hours of tracking game or gathering wild plants were not periods of dull-witted wandering in the wild, but of keenly observant reading and interpreting of signs to which most twenty-first century people would be quite oblivious. Ecologists have noted, with chagrin, that many children and teens today can recognize hundreds of commercial products by brand name, but can identify only a few trees, birds, or plants. We've become increasingly blind to the complex, wild world in which we developed our perceptive capacities, while tragically convincing ourselves that what really matters is the much-improved artificial world we have invented to replace it. Products that will purportedly give us ever greater time-saving, effort-saving convenience and safety surround us, while the world that is actually our only ultimate security fades from our sight.

One of the most primal of all human experiences—having a baby—gave me and my family a revealing sense of just how separated from our origins we have become. When a baby was born in Paleolithic times, we can only speculate about what means the parents may have found to keep the baby alive and safe, and then to help it grow and learn. Infant and child mortality was probably very high. But those who survived infancy had to become very fit and acutely observant at an early age. And of course, fitness and perceptivity in turn provided a survival advantage that continued to develop over thousands of generations. Just as the persistence hunt required physical endurance and patience, tracking and gathering required acute observation and patience. The patience of the hunter-gatherers can still be seen—or felt—in the satisfactions of gardening, the "slow food" movement, meditation, hiking, fishing, bird-watching, and quiet walks in the park, *as well as* long-distance running. And young children seem to take very naturally to those quiet pursuits, if given a chance.

By the time my daughter was born, there were hundreds of products available—none of which had been available to the hunter-gatherers—to make the baby safer and the mother more comfortable. Thirty years later, when *her* baby was due, I accompanied her to a store that sells nothing *but* baby products. I was overwhelmed. I asked the store manager how many different products the store carried, and he cheerfully told me: eighty thousand. He knew them all. But I wondered if he could have identified one-thousandth as many of the plants and animals on which his life—or my grandchild's life—actually depends. Most of those invented products will make babies safer and more comfortable, and even more sedated, but not—as far as I could see—more prepared to undertake a toughening and vigilant journey through life. And as Paul Shepard noted, the kind of high-risk hunt that was both the hunter's greatest danger and his greatest reward will no longer be an option. The "thrill of the kill" already has a barbaric ring, even though it was what kept us going for a hundred times as long as civilization has so far.

The excitement of the finish, then, is not so much a recognition of what has been achieved through the quiet process of training, as it is a primal and ritual responsiveness we feel to the climactic captured moments of those long-forgotten, epic hunts that let us live another day. They are among the most archetypal, hormone-rousing reminders we have that the cycle of life goes on. For a long-distance runner, the end of the race is when you pause for rest before beginning a long and patient preparation for the next race and that sense of rebirth it will bring.

■ ■ ■

At about a mile and a half to go, the road went up what I think was an overpass—though by now I was too fixated on the middle distance ahead of me to really look—then curved right onto a highway, with a lane along the left marked off for the runners with orange cones. Then, up ahead—could it be?—there was the Marine, Tom Hethcoat! He had to have been at least four or five minutes ahead of me a few miles back. But now, suddenly, I was gaining on him, and on another runner just behind him. I let myself, finally, begin to think about the final minutes of the race. Until then, it had seemed too risky. Envisioning the final surge is enormously powerful, but that surge is a bit like the rocket an astronaut uses to return to Earth through heavy gravity—he (or the guy at the controls in Houston) doesn't dare ignite it too soon. It means going anaerobic for the first time in eight hours. The finish is something you've envisioned a thousand times, but now you're girding for the real thing. The real thing is both intense and surprisingly ephemeral. You'll finally have that moment you've dreamed of for months or years, but it will in fact be only a moment.

At about five hundred yards out, officials waved me into a right-hand turn up a short hill. I'd closed further on Hethcoat and the other guy, but wasn't going to catch them. In just a few long seconds, I would crest the hill, see the finish-line banner, and hear the loudspeaker a quarter-mile away. I glanced at my watch, and while it was now a struggle to do even the simplest arithmetic, I could see that this wasn't like the inevitable scene in a movie where the protagonist *barely* defuses the bomb as the clock ticks down, "3 . . . 2 . . . 1 . . ." or where the winning touchdown is scored *just as* the clock runs out. This was real, and I was going to beat the age-group record by about twenty minutes. The record was somewhere around 8:16, and I was about to break eight hours with minutes to spare. Over the last few hundred yards, I summoned up neural memories of the exhilarating last laps of my one-mile runs in high school, over four decades ago, and finally went anaerobic. I sprinted (or at least it felt like that) past the big finish-line clock at 7:55-something. Mike Spinnler, the race director, put a medal around my neck, shouted something exuberant to my unhearing ear, and then it was over. There would be a couple of hours of afterglow and then, like a morning dew, it would be gone.

15

LATE AFTERNOON

The Fading Light

THE MOMENT I'D dreamed of had *come* . . . and minutes later had passed. At 2:55:46 in the afternoon, I had broken the age-division record. Five minutes later, I could hear Mike Spinnler back on the PA mike, heralding the approach of another runner: *"Mich-ael War-di-an!"* Years later I would hear that name again, as Michael Wardian would come back to win the JFK and then go on to place third in the 2009 World 50-kilometer championship in Gibraltar—and then lead the US ultra team to its first world 100K championship in the Netherlands, in 2011—and that year be named the world's Ultrarunner of the Year. By then, I would be hours behind him. In 2001, the arc of his life was rising even as mine was falling, and for this one brief moment our paths had crossed. But right now, I couldn't know that. The sun was still in the sky. I found Sharon and Elizabeth, and this time got hugs I could linger gratefully for.

Later, what I would remember was not just that fleeting satisfaction of the finish, but a reel of moments across the whole experience—the last year of training; the chill of the predawn morning in Boonsboro; the thousands of bare shoulders, arms, and legs of men and women crowding together before the start; the sound of shoes shuffling through leaves on the Appalachian Trail; the sudden fall and crack of knee and elbow on rock; the young Marine who passed me on the towpath an hour or two later and said to me, "You're bleeding, sir"; the unhappy realization that at some point later I must have passed him back and not recognized him and said nothing; the glint of the November sun on the river; the enveloping peace; the ghosts of Americans killing each other in a corn field; the cheering of friendly spectators at Antietam; the creeping fatigue and internal struggle and wandering thoughts and rescuing epiphanies—and *then* the raucous sound of the finish-line PA and that one final minute of validation: seeing the clock and claiming the record, then being swallowed by the finish chute and standing spent as an official collected my ID tag.

A few days after the race, I studied the results on the JFK 50 Mile website and found that, of the 818 runners who had completed the distance before the cut-off, I had finished 49th. I'd finished ahead of four of the seven runners on the top Marines team (the "All-Marines"), five of the seven on the Quantico Marines team, five of the seven on the US Naval Academy team, all seven of the second navy team, and all seven of the army's 82nd Airborne team. Overall, I had out-run 28 of the 35 military runners and had come within a minute and a half of catching one more of the Marines—Tom Hethcoat. I'd finished ahead of 83 of the 104 runners in the race who were under the age of thirty. Among the forty finishers who were sixty or older (about twenty more hadn't made the cutoff), I had finished first and beat the second-place guy by an hour and fifteen minutes.

Then I did a kind of double-take. What I saw on the website was page after page of numbers—the "splits" for each runner (times at Weverton, Antietam, and other aid stations), pace (minutes per mile) at each of those splits, and final times for each runner, plus a plethora of miscellaneous statistics. There were no anecdotes, photos of the runners, videos, or records of what we'd said to each other on the trail. I'd been poring over the numbers for an hour—and it struck me that I'd been tracking pages like these all my life. Suddenly, it seemed that there was something both comical and sad about how seriously I had regarded all these abstract numbers—the sub-eight-hour JFK for the past year, but also the sub-three-hour marathon decades ago, or the 65-second quarter-mile intervals before that, or when I was a kid reading the newspaper and daydreaming, the four-minute mile. The procession of numbers I'd tracked or pursued through the years was like the bones and skeletons sought by anthropologists—provocative relics, suggestive of something momentous, but still only dry relics. I thought abruptly of the Marine telling me back on the towpath that I was bleeding—and my laughing *in appreciation*. I was alive!

In reading over all those stats, I did encounter one small mystery: The runner who finished just ahead of me, right between Tom Hethcoat and me, was listed as Frank Probst. I stared at the list. It wasn't what I remembered at all. I went back and studied the splits, and according to those, I'd been five minutes ahead of Frank at the Dam 4 turnoff onto the road. But mysterious Frank, who could dodge a Boeing 757 and evidently could run like a stealth bomber, had apparently passed me somewhere on the road. I remembered Hethcoat racing past me around eight miles out; maybe Probst had been running in his shadow.

But then, what difference did it make? And anyway, Frank was still in the fifty to fifty-nine age group. All I could do was smile. When I was younger, I had to have answers. Now I knew I could do no more than pursue them. The older I get and the more I learn, the less I know with certainty. And that actually feels right, although I really can't say exactly why.

And that was it: What had happened in this race had been a flesh-and-blood, microcosmic experience of what it is for a tribe of highly evolved humans to be fully functioning on a sheltering planet. It was not a scientific investigation of the persistence-hunting theory, because even modern science, with its painstaking methodologies, is too slow, now, to keep up with the complexity and speed of what is happening in our endurance runners' hearts and lungs—and feet. A supercomputer might be able to beat a grandmaster at chess, but what happens when a man or woman runs across the earth's variegated landscape is a billion times more complex than any chess game. As the physicist Michio Kaku might have assured me on that day he pointed out the limitations of Moore's Law, we humans are "still the man."

In running this race, I was responding to the conundrum that—as our best scientists have tried to make clear—we humans are also *no longer thinking on our feet.* In some respects, the scientists are to blame for the confusion; their reductionist insistence on a methodology that analyzes complex processes by isolating one factor at a time has put us in a position where we are being overwhelmed by the unforeseen and now cascading consequences of our own inventions. When advocates of greater creativity and innovation in the management of our industries and institutions say we need to "think outside the box," they may not question whether the kind of thinking they advocate is still contained by a larger box—the unexamined assumption that inventiveness is always to be found in the future. But if the Industrial Revolution and subsequent telecommunications and biotech revolutions have all happened in just the most recent one-tenth of 1 percent of our evolution, it stands to reason that the our species' capacity to do all that inventing developed before civilization ever began. Stone-age humans and their predecessors didn't have smartphones, but they were smart on their feet, for far longer than we post-industrial people have been, and in ways that we have only begun to grasp.

On November 23, after several days of rest, I went out for my first run since the JFK. I was pleased to find that I had no soreness in my calves. After the marathons I ran in the '60s, my calves were usually so stiff and sore that the only way I could go down steps was backward, using my quads to lower myself flatfooted. Now I was a lot older, but my legs were more resilient than they'd been when I was young, thanks to a few decades of continued learning. There's no fountain of youth, and there's no anti-aging pill, but there is a secret strategy that does work to a remarkable degree, and is free: continuing to learn with an open mind and unobstructed heart.

As I prepared to close the book on my age-sixty JFK and start dreaming about trying it again one day when I was older and wiser, I pondered what President Kennedy might think if he could see our condition today. He might be shocked at the physical obesity, passivity, and poor health of our general population, but fascinated and encouraged by the growing cohort within that population that has taken to heart his claim that physical and mental fitness are interdependent. And it might come to him as a great epiphany that that kind of integrated, or *meta*, fitness, that he knew is so important to the survival of his country, is also interdependent with the health of the planet itself.

But what JFK might find most intriguing and encouraging is the realization that this growing population-within-the-population is moving forward quite independently of the long-dominant power structures of national and global governance, including health governance. Worldwide, a hundred million long-distance runners, and who knows how many other allied communities of mindful people, are steadily, quietly moving toward more enduring, less consuming and corrupting, lifestyles—both as highly independent, self-directed individuals and as consciously interdependent members of their communities, ecosystems, and world.

I could see now that, rather than letting ourselves be blitzed by the juggernaut of the sprint economy, the growing cohort of runners and others who practice individual endurance, patience, and mindful envisioning of the decades ahead might be quietly helping to transform the institutions of that economy from within, even as we are transforming ourselves. Beginning with Clarence DeMar, Ted Corbitt, George Sheehan, and a few others, long-distance runners led the way to a sea change in the medical profession's recognition of how dramatically cardiovascular fitness can reduce the risks of hypertension, diabetes, and heart disease. As if awakening from a long institutional amnesia, a whole phalanx of health-care professions began to grasp the potential benefits—in higher levels of mental fitness, higher quality of life, and dramatically lower health-care costs—of energetically warding off disease rather than passively resigning ourselves to its attacks.

Long-distance running also brought into American life—and increasingly, international life—a very different understanding of *competition* than the kind of winner-takes-all ideology that had dominated all things American for the past half-century. In the 1980s, corporate managers—inspired by members of their own ranks who were running in events like the New York Marathon—began discovering that higher levels of cardiovascular fitness in their executives could dramatically reduce costs incurred due to premature heart attacks, group-health outlays, and sick days. The stereotypical image of a gilded-age industrial mogul—fat guy with a chauffeur and cigar—was obsolete for good, and the successful business man or woman was lean, fit, and often out at 6:00 AM for a run. Deep breathing was essential to sharp thinking.

And, finally, that more enlightened view of competitiveness, which quietly made running the most popular American participant sport in just one generation, and which the football player David Meggyesy explained as our need in *any* sport or endeavor to "strive together or there is no game," clearly began to affect what we know of our relationship to the larger life of the earth.[1] Sustainability is endurance writ large. There are millions of us now who can run a 10K or marathon or even fifty miles over mountain trails without getting out of breath, and then cross the finish line feeling good. I think President Kennedy would have liked our vigor.

POSTSCRIPT: 2012

I AM WRITING this book in the year 2012, over a decade after my 2001 JFK race and seven years after retiring from World-watch Institute to ponder the future of the *human* race. I'm pondering what may now be the ultimate question for us all: *Where do we go now*, when the obstacles we face are even greater than they were for early humans facing vast, unknown territories with only hand implements to hunt or defend themselves with, and only their legs to carry them? Changing climate was undoubtedly a driving force in some of their jour-neys as it now must be for ours, except that for us there are no remaining virgin territories on the planet to go to, and for us the climate change is happening much faster than in the past, thanks to our own blinkered behavior and denial.

A rough logic tells me, then, that our own migration will have to be cultural, not territorial. And paradoxically (which makes it so hard to understand and embrace), it will have to happen with breathtaking speed even as we *let go* of our infatuation with speed and the sprint culture. Like the Green Bay quarterback Aaron Rodgers making his game "slow down" in the 2010 Super Bowl, or good athletes in any sport perceptually slowing the action around them in order to see the game more clearly, we need to slow down to get there faster. I learned in my training for ultras, and for my age-record run at JFK, that I needed not only to pace myself for the long run in terms of external conditions, as an athlete in "the zone" must, but also to slow the turmoil within.

The challenge, in envisioning this course, is that humanity has never faced anything so daunting. The deforestation, drought, erosion, and ecological collapses that brought earlier civilizations to ruin were all regional. Our threat is global. The Black Death, Irish potato famine, Spanish Inquisition, Flu pandemic of 1918, and even the genocides and world wars of the last century, were mostly one-generation decimations. The Inquisition lasted a little longer, and in some respects still continues. But what we face now is an avalanche of dangers that will plague us and our progeny more centuries into the future than I think we can grasp. Meanwhile, what awaits us just around the bend is what Rachel Carson, Ted Taylor, Mikhail Gorbachev, Lester Brown, Paul Ehrlich, and a hundred other pioneers have foreseen—and what millions more of us now can see clearly: We need to be nearing a tipping point.

When President John F. Kennedy was elected in 1960, he may have known, at least intuitively, that science would eventually confirm his belief that "if we fail to encourage physical development and prowess, we will undermine our capacity for thought, for work, and for the use of those skills vital to an expanding and complex America."[1] Today, the same can be said of the whole world. JFK elaborated:

We do not live in a regimented society where men are forced to live their lives in the interest of the state. We are, all of us, free to direct the activities of our bodies as we are to pursue the objects of our thought. But if we are to retain this freedom, for ourselves and for generations to come, then we must also be willing to work for the physical toughness on which the courage and intelligence and skill of man so largely depend.[2]

That kind of toughness is not the brutishness that Thomas Hobbes mistakenly attributed to prehistoric humans, or that dominates our action movies, TV cop shows, or gladiator-style sports now. It is the ability to envision and persevere and sense our connections to the wild world in which our persistence-hunting ancestors evolved, and which some ultra-runners and other practitioners of endurance have begun to rediscover. We need to ask our schools and universities to encourage cross-disciplinary exploration that enables young people to see the critical connections between ecology and sustainable food production, between food and fitness—and, as Kennedy stressed, between our fitness and our ability to think on our feet.

That kind of cross-disciplinary exploration offers students (and later, community leaders or policymakers) a far greater awareness of the "big picture" than they would have found in the narrower study of biology, transportation, physics, or phys ed alone. And, significantly, that big-picture awareness makes more comprehensive use of the kind of wide-ranging perception our hunter-gatherer ancestors developed—the ability to connect the movements of clouds, wind, sun, and seasons with the signs of an animal's movements, the terrain, and the availability of cooperative hunting companions, to assess the prospects of having something to eat that night. Every interdisciplinary field moves us a stride closer to replacing our reductionist science and myopic perception with more integrated, whole-picture views. Maybe the kind of brave, pioneering changes initiated by a few far-seeing individuals decades ago, and now gaining traction, will bring us to a tipping point.

As for me, I've experienced the runner's high so many times that I'm already beyond the tipping point—or at least beyond the *tipsy* point, in the sense that Emily Dickinson had in mind when she wrote:

> *Inebriate of air am I*
> *And debauchee of dew*
> *Reeling, through endless summer days,*
> *From inns of molten blue*[3]

The summer days are no longer endless, as they were when I was young, but running under a sky of molten blue in sunny California, where I now live, is still exhilarating. This fall I'm going back to the JFK 50 Mile again, now in the seventy to seventy-nine division. This time, it may take a bit more than an eight-hour or even a nine-hour day, but I still look forward to a long workday when the work is good.

APPENDIX

NOTES FOR AN ASPIRING ULTRARUNNER

ULTRARUNNING IS NOT separate from the rest of life. It will affect your overall vitality, endurance, and patience, and may also affect your relationships and worldview. You will very likely become less complacent, more questioning, more adventurous, and more reconnected with your lost youth. Ultrarunning won't save the world, but it's a practice of the kinds of skills and outlooks that could ultimately help change the world's course and will almost certainly change yours.

1. Allow Enough Time

In almost anything worthwhile, and especially ultrarunning, rushing to achieve success is a big mistake. Our culture has conditioned us to reflexively expect quick success. But quick success is the artificial, largely illusory, lure of an unsustainable civilization. Most people need eight to twelve months of regular running, averaging thirty to forty miles *or more* per week, to build the basic cardiovascular capacity and endurance needed to run an ultra. Most will already have completed a marathon, or at least have substantial long-distance running experience.

Genetically, all humans are built for running, but culture has separated us from nature and it takes time to readapt. While 30-40 miles per week is a minimum, you'll probably be better off gradually working up to 60-80 mpw. If you are young and have good biomechanics and big dreams, you may be headed for 100 mpw or beyond. But remember, more is not always better. And getting to your maximum mpw as quickly as possible is almost always a mistake. Take your time.

2. Build, Sharpen, Taper

It's good to have a target date in mind—the day of the ultra you'd like to run. That determines when you should aim to reach your "peak"—the highest degree of readiness you can hope to reach in the coming year. Then count backward, allowing a couple of weeks before the race for a "taper" (easing off on the training), and before that two or three weeks of "sharpening" (speed work) to put a little spring in your step. The time left between now and the sharpening is what you have available for building "base"—the accumulation of lots of miles at an easy-to-medium pace. Ideally, you'll have six to eight months or more for base building—developing cardiovascular capacity and endurance. If you don't have at least six months for base, pick a later race. Once you reach your peak, you may be able to hold it for two or three months (and even run another ultra, if you're young and crazy) before needing to back off and rebuild base for the following year.

The basis of the one-year pattern may be the long evolution of our species in environments where climate played a larger role in our lives than it may seem to play now. Persistence hunting may have been more difficult or impossible in winter, necessitating periods of relative inactivity and subsistence on stored food. And the universal biological principle of cycles of rest and stress may also play a role. In any case, most ultrarunners make running a seasonal experience—we train year-round, but consciously prepare to be at our best during certain parts of the year, and to build or recover at others.

Some runners race year-round, incorporating races into the base building while forgoing sharpening and tapering. Year-round competitors also use races as their long training runs. If you're preparing for your first ultra, you might benefit by doing something similar—running a marathon or half-marathon as a training run (*not* as hard as you can), six or seven weeks before your ultra.

In the sharpening phase, starting five or six weeks before the ultra, begin incorporating faster workouts (maybe one the first week, then two a week after that). "Faster" in this context doesn't mean anaerobic running or sprinting, but might involve what I still prefer to call anaerobic-threshold running. Some physiologists don't like the term "anaerobic threshold" because they feel it implies that there's a point at which, as the effort becomes more intense, you shift suddenly from aerobic to anaerobic metabolism—which is not quite what happens. Rather, there's a zone of overlap. These academics prefer the term "lactate threshold," which is defined as the level of intensity or caloric consumption at which the production of metabolic waste is right in balance with the rate at which it is being cleared out. Any faster, and the waste builds up and you can't go more than a minute or two before having to slow down and recover. Experience tells us that workouts right around the lactate threshold (often called "tempo" runs) are the best thing you can do to build endurance, and research confirms it. But threshold running only works if you've done enough base building to support that kind of intensity without breaking down. And it only works if it's done infrequently enough (once or twice a week at most) to allow full recovery between one "fast" day and the next.

To begin your sharpening phase, you might do a warm-up of several miles at an easy pace (always warm up before any fast running), then accelerate to threshold (about as fast as you can keep up for at least five or ten minutes), then ease off for a while and go home. Three or four days later, do it again, only this time, take the threshold part a little farther. Maybe in the second week, do an interval workout— alternating faster-than-threshold surges and slow recovery, say, four times. The next time you do an interval workout, go six surges, and the one after that, eight. By then, you may be ready to taper. All the in-between days should be the same kinds of easy distance running you do in base building. Use whatever mix of threshold running and interval work suits you. Just don't overdo it, because fast running raises the risk of injury. If you feel twinges, back off.

The taper is a period of easing down on mileage and intensity—letting the body get some regeneration before the big day. On the day of the ultra, you want to start out feeling fresh and "hungry" to run, not tired out from all the miles you've been doing. The taper typically takes just a week or two—so if your total mileage the third week before the race is 70 miles, the second week out might be 40 and the last week before the race just 20. These numbers are somewhat arbitrary; your individual condition and ability to listen to your body will guide you on the details.

3. Vary Everything: Distance, Speed, Routes, Terrain, and Mental Engagement

This is a basic principle of biological and ecological health, including the ecology of your own life. For biologists and ecologists, *biodiversity*—both within the genetics of a species and in the complexity of a whole ecosystem—is essential to long-run survival. And for athletes and trainers, *cross-training*—combining the benefits of complementary forms of exercise—is one of the secrets of durability and resistance to injury.

Probably the most basic variable in your training is the distance you run each day. A successful pattern for many runners is to go short to moderate distances (5–10 miles) five days each week, then one day a week go long (15–30 miles). To illustrate the importance of that weekly long run, consider two different patterns, each totaling 60 miles for the week. The first is to run 10 miles a day for six days, then take a day off. The second is to run 8 miles a day for five days, then 20 miles on the sixth. While both yield the same total mileage, the first pattern never takes you past the point where you're running low on muscle glycogen and need to adapt to more efficient fat-burning metabolism for endurance. The second takes you past that point four times a month, or about forty times in the year or so you'll spend training for your ultra. While there's no difference between these two patterns in total mileage, the second one provides a huge advantage in training effect.

Varying *speed* is also important. Here, too, a tried-and-true pattern for most people would be to run at slow-to-medium speeds four to six days a week, and then faster for one or two days. To try running fast more than once or twice a week is to invite injury. "Fast" is a relative term, and in your first year of training for an ultra (review point 2 above), it would be prudent to limit your fastest running to the weeks before the taper, and use more low-key variations of speed during base building. These broad categories ("slow" days, "fast" days) can be further broken down as you gain experience. The "slow to medium" pace can vary from a very lazy lope on some days to the pace you might actually hope to run a 50-kilometer race, on another. Remember, running at ultra race pace doesn't mean you're doing a hard workout, if you're only holding that pace for 8 or 10 miles rather than 50K or 50 miles. When you do intervals (again, not necessary at all during a first year of base-building), there's no need to time them as you would if you were training for the 1,500 or 5,000 meters; what's important is simply to run fast enough to be breathing hard and making your heart beat fast. An alternative to regular intervals might be to run a longer stretch of several miles fast (a "threshold" run as described above), then slow down just long enough to recover before doing another several miles fast.

A third alternative is what Scandinavian athletes call *fartlek*—highly irregular shifts of speed within a single run so that you're trying to "surprise" your body and build its resilience and adaptability along with its aerobic capacity. The logic of these patterns is that if you train your body to run fairly often at faster-than-race pace, then "dropping down" to race pace will enable you to feel very comfortable at that pace on the day of the big race. In the fast-pace training, rather than rely on stopwatches, heart monitors, or other techno-assists, practice relying on your own developing ability to "listen to your body." With practice, you won't need electronic monitors to tell you what's happening with your heart, lungs, hormones, and metabolic waste. And in the long run, it's better if you don't. You do value independence, don't you?

Varying *routes* (and thus *terrain*) is important for both physical and psychological reasons. Uphill and downhill running put different stresses on the muscles and tendons, and both differ from running on the flat. A runner I know who had no hills near his home trained for running a mountain ultra by doing long sessions on a treadmill raised to steep-climb settings. He thought that as long as he could handle the climbs, the descents would be no problem. But when he ran the race, the miles-long descents were murder on his quadriceps, which get the lion's share of downhill braking. Unfortunately, treadmills don't have steep downhill settings. If you don't have hills or mountains near home that are comparable to those you'll encounter in your race, you can train just about as well by running up-and-down repeats of a smaller hill. But again, try not to use just one route. Different grades of climbing or descent, like different speeds, use different combinations of muscle fibers. In training, run as many different hills, of different steepness, as possible. And for similar physiological reasons on a more "micro" level, seek out different surfaces as well. Pine-needle paths, dirt, gravel, grass, and pavement each put different stresses on the feet and legs (and even on the core muscles used for balance), and you need to feel at home with all of them when you race.

As for *mental engagement*, experienced runners often distinguish between "associative" running, in which you are focused on all the physical and environmental factors affecting your performance, and "dissociative" running, in which you're not consciously paying attention to the running but are letting your mind wander. Both have their place. It's important to sometimes focus on the running itself, so that you are well attuned to the progress of your conditioning and so that you can consciously practice (or "visualize") racing conditions. But there are also times when it's important to let running be an escape from the stresses of the workplace or home, or our troubled world. On some days it may be better for your mental and physical health to let yourself recall what you said in a conversation that's bugging you, and then fantasize about what you'd *like* to have said, than to be thinking about your stride length or tempo. The more practiced you become, the more the running can take care of itself for hours at a time, while your mind takes care of business.

There's also a kind of engagement that is neither associative nor dissociative, but an integration of both—occasioned by a run in a beautiful place, or past an inspiring scene. If you come over a mountain pass and see an amazing cloud formation and feel your spirit lift, it's a chance to feel your body lifting at the same time; you can be physically aware of being light on your feet and psychologically energized by the scene. It's especially rewarding to integrate both physical and mental experience with the environment you are traversing. That's a big reason why millions of people in the past twenty years have shifted from the roads to the trails—and why most ultras now are on trails.

4. Balance Stress and Rest

This is tricky and complex. Taking time to rest is *not a matter of compromise.* You don't compromise anything by seeking the right balance. Movies about heroic warriors perpetuate the idea that the harder you can train without collapsing, the stronger you will be. Yes, it's basic physiology that stressing a muscle in a workout tears it down a little and stimulates it to grow back stronger. That's true of all physiological systems and mental skills. But the "growing back" part is too easily neglected. In any exercise, you can reach a point beyond which there aren't enough hours left in the night to fully recover before the next day—so the next day's workout begins with *less* muscle or resilience than the day before, and the training effect begins to reverse. Symptoms of improper balance between stress and rest include a "stale" or "flat" feeling, a slump in performance, and then—inevitably, sooner or later—illness or injury. And if you don't learn, you could experience burnout and permanent injury.

Part of the complexity is that different kinds of exercise require different amounts of recovery. Speed work requires more recovery time between sessions than slow base building. It may be counterintuitive, but twelve quarter-mile intervals totaling just three fast miles (or six if you count the alternating slow laps), may need three times as much rest between sessions as longer but slower 10-milers do. Similarly, intense weight-lifting routines require two or three times as much rest between sessions as sit-ups.

Another complexity is that physical exercise is not the only source of stress in your life, so it's not the only stress you have to take into consideration in finding optimal rest and regeneration. Ever since the pioneer endocrinologist Hans Selye began his research on the "stresses of life" almost a century ago, we've understood that while such varied experiences as financial trouble, a car crash, the death of a spouse, a new baby, or the planning for a wedding are all very different, their effects on an individual can add up. A runner who is coping with heavy stress at work or at home, whether emotional, mental, or physical, may not be able to carry as much workload in his or her training as one who feels relaxed and on top of the world. On the other hand, if you've already built some endurance as a runner, you can probably handle more stress in your life as a whole than you could if you were sedentary. Again, the ideal regimen is to find a balance between the cumulative stress of everything that's happening, including the running, and the amount of rest (sleep, days off, easy runs) needed to keep building endurance.

5. Practice Form

Here's where a lot of even very experienced ultrarunners fall short. They got to be what they are—quite competent at getting through a 50K or 100-mile race—by learning the arts of patience and mental toughness, and by doggedly doing the mileage. Yet they run with handicaps and miss out on a big part of what could help them run faster and more enjoyably. Watch a random group of ultrarunners in action, and they look healthy, happy, gnarly, and game, but not especially athletic.

One of the great attractions of spectator sports like basketball or soccer, or of Olympic sports like gymnastics and swimming, is the wonder of the human body in motion. Arguably, there is nothing more beautiful on earth, because there is nothing more complex, and when all the complexities are in synch—in "the zone"—it's thrilling to watch. And, for the athlete, a thrill to experience. More generally, beyond sport, it's this most amazing of nature's wonders that gives us the pleasures of dancing and the integration of body movement with music. Life *is* movement.

Running will be more enjoyable—and your performances more satisfying—if you practice your movement the way a swimmer or basketball player or dancer does. First, as you run, your body should be vertical, not leaning forward. For generations, cartoonists and logo designers have depicted running as an act of tilting forward, but in the real world that would result in falling down on your face. (The only exception is the start of a sprint, when gravity is actually employed as a momentary boost to initial forward propulsion for a few yards, with the legs moving at maximum anaerobic speed to "catch up" with the torso, and even then the sprinter is fully upright within ten yards.) Second, it's important not to "cheat" on the verticality by sagging into a "C" shape, as many joggers and slower runners (especially older ones) do, with their heads appearing to be properly aligned over their feet but their butts and hips hanging behind them. The result is that, while the C-shaped runner doesn't fall on his face, his lower torso is perpetually struggling to keep pace with the knees and chest, and there's no forward momentum. The way to remedy this is to focus on keeping your hips forward and your back straight, not slumped. Third, your feet should point straight forward, so that you're not wasting energy or inviting injury with excessive lateral motion. Recreational runners can sometimes be spotted jogging with feet splayed so far outward that the knees are thrown awkwardly inward—increasing the risk of injury to both feet and knees, not to mention expending so much energy that long-distance running would be out of the question except for a masochist. Fourth, the arms should be swinging forward and back, fairly vertically like the body (not with elbows poking horizontally out to the side), and fairly loose. Practice checking to make sure your shoulders are relaxed, not clenched. Fifth, keep the head fairly still, not wobbling left and right as if tethered to the arms. The head is where the sense of balance is seated. While you're running on rough terrain, your legs and hips may make continuous complex movements to *keep* the balance, but it's the head's job to guide these movements by maintaining an independent, relatively unwavering forward track relative to the horizon.

These basics can't convey the real complexity of good running form, however. They can help you avoid or correct gross mistakes or misconceptions, but the best way to acquire good form may be simply to observe outstanding runners and—if you observe them often enough—to subconsciously incorporate what they're doing into your own form. This is what kids do when they watch elite athletes in a stadium or on TV. High school basketball players have better moves today than they did half a century ago, not just because they're better coached, but because they've spent more hours watching NBA and NCAA games. That's not to say personal coaching by an expert in the biomechanics of running might not help, but simply watching great athletes can do wonders for getting your ancient running instincts activated. The best coaching you can get might be watching videos of great marathon runners or—if you can find them—ultrarunners like Scott Jurek, Ann Trason, or Michael Wardian.

6. Neither a Loner nor a Groupie Be

A healthy and fit human is a social animal. We survived our evolution for a hundred millennia by working and cooperating in small groups: the family and tribe, and particularly the hunting party—the original cross-country team. If your cross-country team consists of the Olympic 5,000-meter champion and six C-shaped joggers, it will lose every meet! The scoring of cross-country is based on the recognition that at its roots, this is a team endeavor. Since humans could not have successfully hunted mammoths as lone heroes, they had to chase down their prey in packs, the way wolves do. So, it's in our genes to run in groups. And most long-distance runners do at least some of their training (as well as all of their racing, of course) in groups. Lone heroes have been romanticized in our cultural consciousness by solitary comic-book superheroes, cowboy heroes like the Lone Ranger, and action-movie characters who are on the run from their erstwhile colleagues at the CIA and have to survive by their wits. But the biological reality is that humans are interdependent.

On the other hand, in evolution, cooperation was essential, but limited by nature: The hunting party provided mutual protection, but if one member sat down in a funk and refused to continue, he probably got eaten by a lion. His funk genes weren't perpetuated. And in the world we have inherited, society functions best if we cooperate but also continue to carry our own weight. We are *inter*dependent but also *in*dependent.

For the ultrarunner, to keep that sense of independence strong, it's helpful to do a significant amount of running alone. If you can run with a companion or group once or twice a week, that's good. But chances are, you spend most of your time both at work and at home interacting with others, so you probably don't lack for social experience. What you may not have so much of is true independence. A few days a week of solitary running can do wonders for that. To practice feeling independent and self-sufficient on the trail is not just a boon to your running; it is one of the great rewards. Take your water bottle, but leave the GPS and smartphone at home. At least part of the time, it's important to connect with the air, forest, wildlife, and the signals emanating from your own body, not just to chat with companions.

7. Check Your Gear

Long-distance running is a major sport (*what?*) but doesn't require a major investment in equipment.

This demands clarification. TV sports fans might find my designation of running as a major sport ludicrous, because in the mainstream media it isn't even a *minor* sport—it is virtually nonexistent. But as measured not in numbers of spectators but in numbers of actual participants, it may come as a surprise to many TV producers that running is America's most popular sport. In a recent survey, the Sporting Goods Manufacturing Association found that more than forty-nine million Americans run regularly, as compared with about eleven million who play baseball and eleven million who play basketball.

The primary reason for the huge disparity between participation and media coverage is, of course, the fact that running is not a spectator sport, and in the current culture of high-speed thrills and highlights it can't attract large audiences. And even if it could, the cost of taking TV cameras and crews up single-track mountain trails would be prohibitive. But a second reason is that ultrarunning is a minimalist activity; it doesn't sell the gargantuan volumes of equipment that other sports do. It doesn't offer advertisers the same cybernetic spectacles of athletes' bodies bedecked in superhero-like uniforms, helmets, pads, gloves, and shoes, and wielding bats, rackets, sticks, and clubs, as well as skis, skates, boards, bicycles, and even motorcycles, power boats, parachutes, and racing cars.

As a long-distance runner, you don't need any of that stuff, except the shoes—and a fair number of minimalists in recent years have even tried going without the shoes. On the other hand, there's a short list of functional equipment, including shoes, that you will find useful. And because of the greater demands for nutrient replenishment and rehydration at beyond-marathon distances, you'll need several pieces of equipment that a marathoner or 10K runner won't normally need.

Running shoes are your most important equipment, no matter what barefoot advocates might say. Bare feet might work on a nicely groomed dirt or pine-needle path in the park, but not on a road shoulder where there will be broken glass, or on a trail where you'll encounter thousands of rocks, ruts, roots, and maybe an occasional snake. You *don't* need high-tech, $150 or $200 shoes, and they don't have to be "trail" shoes, even if all your running is on trails—good road-running shoes are usually fine. On the other hand, don't buy shoes that are cheap knockoffs of respected brands but that have prices too good to be true. A good rule of thumb: Don't buy shoes that cost less than $50, which too often turn out to be bricks. Brands that offer good long-distance running shoes include (in alphabetical order) Adidas, Asics, Brooks, Montrail, Mizuno, New Balance, Nike, Reebok, and Saucony. There may be others, but ask a salesperson who is himself or herself a runner before making a choice. The features to look for are (1) durability, (2) a strong, roomy toe-box (to protect your toes when you kick a rock), (3) enough cushioning to help compensate for the fact that it's been at least ten thousand years since our species ran barefoot in the wild, (4) flexibility (bend the shoe in half; if it's hard to bend, it might be passable for walking, but not for running), and, perhaps most important, (5) a very comfortable fit, with room for the toes to wiggle. Be sure to ask the salesperson about durability, especially at the outer corner of the heel (where most of us touch down, and wear is greatest), since that's the one thing you can't see for yourself in a store or online. Don't buy separate "racing" shoes for your race; run your ultra in the same shoes you train in.

Shorts and *shirts* are easier. They need only to be comfortable and loose enough to permit unrestricted leg and arm motion (and air cooling), and made of a quick-drying (or "wicking") material, so you won't be lugging around pounds of sweat.

A *hat* is *de rigueur* for an ultrarunner, both to protect against hours of UV exposure and to provide a visor when running into the sun. A baseball-style hat is perfect, if it has mesh ventilation for sweat evaporation and cooling. If you're rich, buy *two* hats—a white one for maximum sun reflection in summer, and a black one for solar heat-absorption on a cold day (or for going on a running date with a Goth). If you live or race in a place where there's serious freezing, a knit hat is best because you need to protect your ears.

A *water bottle* (or other water-carrying system) is essential for an ultrarunner. Most popular is a bottle you carry in your hand, held by a comfortable strap so there's no muscular tension. Another option is a belt that carries one or two bottles (or four small ones) at the small of the back. A third option is a Camelbak, with which you can carry a large quantity of water (and ice, if you like) in a backpack-like container, and which you drink from through a tube. I've never used one of those (I prefer the hand bottle, or a combination of hand bottle and single-bottle belt), and all I can say about the Camelbak is that if the runner just ahead or behind you has filled it with ice cubes, the sound of the cubes slamming back and forth with each step he takes on what would otherwise be a quiet trail can drive you crazy.

In very cold climates, you'll also need a running suit, and/ or a combination of tights and jacket. The most important thing here is that the gear be made of a light, high-tech, quick-drying material (lest your sweat accumulate in the fabric and freeze), and that it be vented to let the heat you generate escape. You might also want a water-repellent, ventilated rain suit or jacket. But don't ever run in something like one of those slickers or waterproof outfits you see firefighters in, because without adequate ventilation or "breathing," the heat buildup from your body's metabolism—even in cool weather—can be fatal.

So: *shoes, shorts, shirt, hat*—plus whatever you need for *hydration* and for cold or rainy weather. It's best to buy all of these things at a shop that specializes in running gear or at a running expo. (Almost every major road race or marathon these days has an expo the day before, with lots of reputable vendors.) Avoid big chain sporting-goods stores, where a big part of the inventory is golf clubs, guns, ammo, and camping stoves, and where whatever running shoes or water bottles they have may not be designed specifically for serious long-distance runners.

8. Be Cautious About Techno-Assists

Any human enterprise can be corrupted—even something as unpoliticized and relatively uncommercialized as ultrarunning. There's a risk that the increasing popularity of carry-along technologies for long-distance runners will begin to erode the very attributes that make ultrarunning the uniquely strengthening and enlightening experience it is.

You may already have decided that one of the reasons you're drawn to this sport is that what you do in an ultra is something *you* control, interdependently with other people but independently of anyone else's manipulation. Government agencies, corporations, or media may strongly restrict or control how you travel through airports, behave on airplanes, drive and park on public streets, buy drugs, enter courthouses, hospitals, or office high-rises, run a business, pay for health care, or pay taxes. Along with all the restrictions and regulations, you get lots of security, safety, subsidies, and assistance.

When you run 50 kilometers or 50 miles or 100 miles, you're on your own—and about as free as a modern human can be. It's hugely challenging to be on your own in a difficult endeavor, but edifying and exhilarating if you succeed.

The problem is that over the past half-century, we've become increasingly enamored with—and dependent on—new technologies designed to relieve us of tasks we once did with our bodies and brains. In the 1950s, washing machines relieved women (who were expected to do all the laundry in those days) of the need to wash clothes by hand. Power mowers spared men (who were expected to do the yard work) the effort of pushing a hand mower. Since then, the aids have proliferated to the point that virtually every basic function of the body, and many functions of the brain as well, have been relieved of the work they once did as their contribution to survival. Personal mobility, lifting and carrying, communication, observation, calculation, physical defense, food processing, waste disposal, and monitoring of physiological conditions have been automated. Not everything we do has been automated, but the trend is relentless. If a doctor wants you to provide a stool sample, you may still have to do that manually. But if you do it in a public or hospital restroom, you may not have to manually turn the faucet—a motion sensor will do it for you. And now, I have read, a Japanese company has designed a toilet for your home that will collect your poop on a regular basis, analyze it, and automatically report any abnormalities to the local health department. Big Brother under your bottom, so to speak.

The Orwellian toilet is an exception, but most other techno-aids have been introduced to us with such fanfare that we too easily overlook how extensively they have subverted our self-sufficiency, strength, and independence as individuals. When a muscle isn't used, it atrophies. And so does the brain. Mental passivity is evidently one of the factors in Alzheimer's disease or dementia. As noted earlier in this book, recent research in England found that heavy reliance on GPS can cause shrinking of the part of the brain responsible for mental mapping.

For ultrarunners, the risk in this trend is that our culturally inculcated acceptance of techno-assists for all we do (think smartphone apps) will begin eroding the independence that makes our sport what it is. The pioneer running doctor George Sheehan urged the runner to "listen to your body"— to become attuned to all the internal signals that allow us to monitor and adjust our pace, hydration, refueling, and so on. But now we have devices that can do those things for us— GPS-based wrist watches that monitor heart rate, oxygen uptake, lactate threshold, pace, body fat, and the distance you've run. There's nothing inherently wrong with such devices, but if they shortcut the work of running (and remember that self-monitoring is an essential part of that work), excessive reliance on them may be too much like taking a shortcut in a race.

We can't condemn technologies altogether, because we need the cushioning and toe-boxes in our running shoes, and we need stopwatches or finish-line clocks for timing. But with performance-enhancing aids, where do we draw the line? If we accept performance-enhancing heart-rate and lactate-threshold monitors, do we also accept performance-enhancing drugs?

This isn't a question for race directors or USA Track & Field or government regulators. It's very much a question for you. If one of the great appeals of ultrarunning is the sense of extraordinary independence it bestows, any intervention that increases your *de*pendence should give you pause.

9. Rethink Food and Fitness—and the Meaning of Patience

You already know that a long-distance runner is much slower than a sprinter—but lasts much longer. You may also be familiar with the concept of "slow food"—the nutritional and philosophical opposite of fast food. "Slow" running and "slow" food are closely connected. With both, quick gratification is out of the question. Good nutrition for a distance runner, like the cardiovascular endurance training that it fuels, is a gradual process taking place over months or years. Supplying the nutrients for optimal base building takes—and teaches—considerable patience. In the long-term relationship between food and ultra-fitness, here are three basic principles to keep in mind:

1. *Good food is not about boosting performance on race day or the night before.* Ultrarunning is not about taking shortcuts. Good fueling is important, but not nearly as important as good nutrition in the months (and if possible, years) before the run. Food for performance can't be mainly a last-day thing any more than building cardiovascular capacity can. What you eat over the long term has far more effect than what you eat at a carbo-loading dinner or aid station.

2. *All food is made up of living organisms, and all complex organisms get their nutrients from other organisms.* We humans can only live by consuming other living (or recently living) things, whether animal or plant. For hundreds of millennia, that meant hunting or gathering; now it means farming. It means that even if you're a Buddhist, Quaker pacifist, or Lascaux Cave artist who reveres

animals, you can only live if you accept some form of taking other life to sustain your own. What food is *not* is any of the hundreds of petrochemical preservatives, dyes, artificial flavors or colors, stabilizers, or emulsifiers found in thousands of highly processed products that Americans now eat. Many of those products, combining chemicals with highly refined sugars, fats, and salt, have been heavily implicated in what nutritionists now call "lifestyle diseases"—heart disease, cancer, diabetes, and many more.

3. *Defensive dieting invites failure.* If your main motivation for choosing particular foods is that you fear being overweight or being at high risk of heart attack or cancer, you're playing a losing game. It's like a football coach having his players expend all their energy trying to stop the other team from scoring. Most sports coaches advise that it's a big mistake to just focus on trying *not to lose,* as opposed to focusing on doing really well. You need offense, too!

What's missing in these defensive reactions is a seeking of food that doesn't just help prevent malnutrition or illness, but can actively make a person *more well,* and by extension *more fit.* And that, in turn, affects the health of the earth in myriad ways. For example, consider the links between meat eating and climate change. We evolved as long-distance-running hunters who ran down animals for food, so meat eating is in our genes. But it's significant that 99 percent of that evolution occurred during a period when the human population was very small and stable. It is now huge and growing by more than seventy million people a year—the equivalent of a hundred more New York Cities or Cairos in just the next decade. Today, we still get protein from meat, but producing a pound of protein from meat also produces about eight times as much global-warming gas as producing a pound of protein from plant sources.

Without fellow humans, there's no foot race. Without a healthy planet, there's no *human* race. Philosophically and physically, you can't separate your running from your larger world without paying a heavy penalty. If you do, your enjoyment of the running—and as a result, your performance and longevity—will probably be stunted. It's not surprising, then, that many ultrarunners, including some of the best in the world, have adopted natural-foods diets. It's also not surprising, given the massive changes in the ecology of food that civilization has wrought, that some of the world's top ultrarunners are now vegetarians.

This is not an argument for vegetarianism. You can be a happy and successful runner and a meat eater, too. What's most important from a nutritional perspective is to find foods that are free of heavy processing and as close as possible on your plate to the way they grow in the wild. At least eat foods made with whole grains rather than white flour. Get brown rice rather than white. Raw vegetables more than cooked. If you eat chicken or eggs, get free-range, rather than chickens or eggs produced in poop-ridden pens (the standard industry practice), dosed with antibiotics as required to get permitting for such conditions. If you eat fish, eat small, wild-caught fish rather than farm-raised ones fattened with monoculture feeds and antibiotics (and in the case of salmon, made to look wild with artificial orange color). And for anything that you eat from agricultural sources, try to keep it organic (rather than produced with chemical pesticides and fertilizers) as much as possible. People often complain about organic foods costing more, but over a lifetime, the added cost could well be dwarfed by what you will save in medical costs down the road.

10. Be at Home in the Wild

A common failing of long-distance runners, especially on solo training runs, is the desire to get back home. You're out on a bleak winter day, and you imagine being back in your living room, snug with a big sandwich, chips, and TV. Do you have a fireplace? Even worse. Or, it's a hot summer day and the water in your bottle has gone tepid, and you anticipate getting back home and pouring cold juice over a tall glass of ice cubes, then exercising twenty seconds of patience to let the drink chill before beginning to sip.

OK, the twenty seconds of patience could be a good sign— you're learning. But the real problem here is your subconscious, default feeling about "home."

This is not to suggest there's anything wrong with your desire to get back to house and hearth. But if that desire causes you to cut the run short, or skip it on a day when the weather looks bad, then there may be something important missing in your feel for the place where you're running.

Our species evolved in the wild, and for every century we've been civilized, there were ten centuries or more when we lived in the wild, and *that* was home—and that deeper sense of home is still in our DNA. One way to look at it is to consider that just as dogs are domesticated from wolves, modern humans are domesticated from nomadic hunter-gatherers. Give a healthy dog a chance, and it will revel in being able to go for a run in fields or woods—and, significantly, it will most likely exhibit more pleasure with that outing than with any time it spends in the living room or dog house. A dog that is too dog-show domesticated is a sad thing. Ditto a human who can't reconnect with our primordial love of the wild—the source of all our adventure, discovery, and sustenance for hundreds of thousands of years before we had sitcoms, spectator sports, or potato chips.

The key is to see the wild not as lonely or sinister, as commonly depicted in TV shows or movies, but as a realm where you can be comfortable and self-reliant and free, and where you belong. Once the wild feels like home, you're home free to be an ultrarunner.

NOTES

CHAPTER 2

1 Clarence DeMar, *Marathon* (Brattleboro, Vermont: Stephen Daye Press, 1937), 26–27.

2 John F. Kennedy, "The Soft American," *Sports Illustrated,* December 26, 1960, http://sportsillustrated.cnn.com/vault/article/magazine/MAG1134750/1/index.htm.

3 "Computer Gamers Have 'Reactions of Pilots but Bodies of Chain Smokers,'" *The Telegraph,* June 7, 2010, http://www.telegraph.co.uk/technology/video-games/7808860/Computer-gamers-have-reactions-of-pilots-but-bodies-of-chain-smokers.html.

4 Kennedy, "The Soft American."

5 Joe Henderson, Running Commentary, *Running Times,* September 1987, 6.

CHAPTER 3

1 Nathaniel G. Plant and Gary B. Griggs, "Interactions Between Nearshore Processes and Beach Morphology Near a Seawall," *Journal of Coastal Research* 8, no. 1 (1992): 183–200.

2 Joseph Ellis, DPM, FACFO, "Shoe Selection Guide," 15–19; "The 1980 Models: How They Rate," 20–24; and "Methodology," 27, *Running Times,* October 1979.

CHAPTER 4

1 Alex Ayres, "Body and Brain: The Impacts of Aerobic Running on Intelligence," *Running Times,* August 1982, 21 (emphasis added).

2 Ibid.

3 Alex Ayres, "If They Don't Run, They Don't Eat," *Running Times,* March 1977, 13.

4 Ibid.

5 John Annerino, "Running Against Time," *Running Times*, May 1984, 23.

6 David Carrier, A. K. Kapor, Tausko Kimura, Martin K. Nickels, Satwanti, Eugene C. Scott, Joseph K. So, and Erik Trunkaus, "The Energetic Paradox of Human Running and Hominid Evolution," *Current Anthropology* 25, no. 4 (August–October 1984).

7 Twenty years after the publication of Carrier's seminal article (note 6 above), Bramble and Harvard University professor of human biological evolution Daniel Lieberman coauthored a landmark confirmation of the running-man theory: D.M. Bramble and D.E. Lieberman, "Endurance Running and the Evolution of *Homo*," *Nature* 432, no. 7015 (November 2004).

8 Joan Benoit, *Running Tide* (New York: Alfred A. Knopf, 1987), 21–22.

9 Christopher McDougall, *Born to Run: A Hidden Tribe, Superathletes, and the Greatest Race the World Has Never Seen* (New York: Knopf, March 2011), 223.

10 Dennis Bramble, email message to author, October 19, 2011. The email noted: "I recognized your name from back in my earliest days of becoming interested in human running and its evolutionary implications. I subscribed to *Running Times* for a time while you were still editor. I thought your publication the best ready source of data on distance performance vs. age and gender, a subject that continues to interest me rather deeply, especially as it may relate to larger issues in human evolution."

11 Herb Mann, "Mozart the Runner," *Running Times*, September 1982, 29.

CHAPTER 5

1 Scott Nelson, *Steel Drivin' Man: John Henry, the Untold Story of an American Legend*, (Oxford: Oxford University Press, 2008), 32.

2 Ibid. (emphasis added).

3 *Morris County* (NJ) *Daily Record* (February 15, 1963).

4 Paul Kiczek, "The 50-Mile Hike Phenomenon: a Look Back at the New Frontier of Fitness," *50milehikers* (blog), November 13, 2010, http://50milehikers.wordpress.com.

5 Ibid.

6 Ibid.

7 Ibid.

8 Ibid.

CHAPTER 6

1 Henry A. Bent, "Interface Series: Energy and Exercise," *Journal of Chemical Education* 55, no. 12 (December 1978), 796.

2 "Pocket Movement," Alamo City Quarterback Camp, http://alamocityqbcamp.com/?page=Pocket%20Movement.

3 Mike McCarthy, quoted in Kareem Copeland, "Fate of Super Bowl XLV Rested with Green Bay Quarterback Aaron Rodgers," http://packersnews.greenbaypressgazette.com, February 9, 2011.

4 Steve Taylor, *Making Time: Why Time Seems to Pass at Different Speeds and How to Control It* (London: Icon, 2005).

5 Roy S. Johnson, "Slow Your Roll," *Men's Fitness*, February 2011, 8.

CHAPTER 7

1 Paul Shepard, *The Tender Carnivore and the Sacred Game* (Athens: University of Georgia Press, 1973).

2 Ibid., 7.

3 Jim Burgess, "Spectators Witness History at Manassas," *Hallowed Ground Magazine*, Spring 2011, http://www.civilwar.org/hallowed-ground-magazine/spring-2011/spectators-witness-history-at.html.

4 Theodore B. Taylor, "Circles of Destruction," *Bulletin of the Atomic Scientists* 52, no. 1 (January 1996).

CHAPTER 8

1 Thomas Hobbes, *Leviathan, or the Matter, Forme, and Power of a Common-Wealth, Ecclesiasticall and Civil* (London: Andrew Crooke, 1651).

2 Jared Diamond, "The Worst Mistake in the History of the Human Race," *Discover*, May 1987, 64–66.

3 Ibid.

4 Ibid.

5 George Sessions, foreword to *The Tender Carnivore and The Sacred Game* (Athens: University of Georgia Press, 1973), ix.

6 Shepard, *The Tender Carnivore*, 83–84.

7 Wendell Berry, *The Unsettling of America: Culture and Agriculture* (Sierra Club Books, 1996).

8 David Carrier, "The Energetic Paradox of Human Running and Hominid Evolution," *Current Anthropology* 15, no. 4 (August–October 1984), 483.

9 Dennis Bramble and Daniel Lieberman, "How Running Made Us Human," *Nature* 432, no. 7015 (November 18, 2004).

10 Benoit, *Running Tide*, 27.

CHAPTER 10

1 American Council on Exercise, *Lifestyle & Weight Management Consultant Manual.*
2 Ed Ayres, "What Happened at Herndon," *Running Times,* November 1980, 10–16.
3 Ibid., 11.
4 Ibid., 12.
5 John F. Rocket, "After Herndon: How a Boy's Life Was Saved" (letter to the editor), *Running Times,* February 1981, 10.

CHAPTER 11

1 John L. Parker Jr., "The Tee Vee Olympics," in *Runners & Other Dreamers* (Tallahassee: Cedarwinds, 1989), 17.
2 John Keats, "Ode on a Grecian Urn," *Annals of the Fine Arts* 15 (January 1820).
3 Maria A. I. Aberg, Nancy L. Pederson, Kjell Toren, Magnus Svartengren, Björn Bäckstrand, Tommy Johnsson, Christina M. Cooper-Kuhn, N. David Åberg, Michael Nilsson, and H. Georg Kuhn, "Cardiovascular Fitness Is Associated with Cognition in Young Adulthood," *Proceedings of the National Academy of Sciences* 106, no. 99 (December 8, 2009).

CHAPTER 12

1 John Parker Jr., "To Imagine Victory," in *Runners & Other Dreamers* (Tallahassee: Cedarwinds, 1989), 106.
2 Henry Kendall, "World Scientists' Warning to Humanity" (Cambridge, Massachusetts: Union of Concerned Scientists [UCS], November 18, 1992). Signed by 1,700 senior scientists including 104 Nobel Prize winners in the sciences.
3 American Museum of Natural History, "National Survey Reveals Biodiversity Crisis—Scientific Experts Believe We Are in Midst of Fastest Mass Extinction in Earth's History—Crisis Poses Major Threat to Human Survival; Public Unaware of Danger" (press release), (New York: American Museum of Natural History: April 20, 1998).

CHAPTER 13

1 DeMar, *Marathon,* 59.
2 Benoit, *Running Tide,* 19.
3 José Ortega y Gasset, *Meditations on Hunting,* translated by Howard Wescott (New York: Charles Scribner's Sons, 1972).

4 David Meggyesy, personal communications with author
   including emails on June 11, 2010, and February 13 and 15,
   2011.

CHAPTER 14

1 Jim Ferstle, Phil Stewart, and Ed Ayres, "New York's Epic Race,"
   and Steve Kelly, "A TV Viewer Loses All Control," *Running
   Times*, January 1984, 22–28.

CHAPTER 15

1 David Meggyesy, email messages to author, February 13 and 15,
   2011.

POSTSCRIPT

1 John F. Kennedy, "The Soft American."
2 Ibid.
3 Emily Dickinson, "I Taste a Liquor Never Brewed," *Selected
   Poems* (New York: Dover Publications, 1990), 3.

ACKNOWLEDGMENTS

I COULD NEVER have reached the finish line for this book without the extraordinary serendipity that brought me to my literary agent Stephany Evans and, through her, to my publisher Matthew Lore. Both she and he went far beyond the normal call of duty for their professions to help make this book happen—as did the extraordinary teams who work for them.

Fellow runners who have helped prepare me for this project over the years—some of them without even knowing it—include the kids I coached at the George School and Swarthmore College in the 1960s (these "kids" now in their late sixties) and my teammates with the Central Jersey Track Club and Washington Sports Club in the 1970s. Thanks to Bob Harper, my DC neighbor and frequent running partner, who introduced me to ultrarunning—and to the mystique of the JFK 50 Mile.

I'll always appreciate the support I got from my partners in the founding of *Running Times*, Phil Stewart and Rick Platt, both of whom ran faster marathons than I and taught me a lot about endurance not only on the road but in our epic, all-night efforts to get the magazine to the printer each month. Thanks to my brothers Gene and Alex, both of them writers, who have given me the kinds of unflagging sympathy and support we writers sometimes urgently need. Alex joined our little staff at *Running Times* soon after our launch, fresh from a stint as editor of the *Harvard Lampoon,* and his influence helped me appreciate the value of punctuating serious discourse with good humor. This book tackles a subject of potentially tragic and universal consequence, yet sometimes there's only a fine line between tragedy and farce. Will civilization triumph, or will it fall on its face?

And then there's my older brother Bob, who first brought me into the world of environmental research and introduced me to the concept of *industrial metabolism,* a concept he originated in the 1970s and which had an epiphanic impact on my thinking about human endurance.

In recounting events that may better prepare us for the future by clarifying our long-forgotten past, I've been inspired by some of the pathbreaking scientists of human evolution—David Carrier and Dennis Bramble at the University of Utah and Daniel Lieberman at Harvard. Any mistakes in my many speculations about our evolutionary past are mine, not theirs.

Several progressive communities, in particular, have inspired me during the half-century I spent preparing my feet, legs, cerebrum, hippocampus, and carotid artery, among other parts, for the one-day adventure of a lifetime this book recounts:

Early trackers of the links between endurance and sustainability— people who could think on their feet and think *with* their feet: Bill McKibben, Lester R. Brown, Roger Brown, Bernd Heinrich, David Kayser, Tony Rossmann, and Curtis Runyan, to name a few.

Runners who have especially inspired me over the years: Ruth Anderson, Joan Benoit, Fred Best, Ted Corbitt, John Creighton, Ron Delany, Clarence deMar, Scott Jurek, Yiannis Kouros, Carlos Lopes, George Sheehan, and Ann Trason.

ACKNOWLEDGMENTS

Visionary groups: Buddhists, Quakers, Universalist Unitarians, anti-war activists, environmental activists, Athletes for Peace, the Road Runners Club of America, the Society for Ecological Economics, and the Union of Concerned Scientists.

Good friends who have supported and encouraged me through the thick and thin of this trek: Leslie Ayres, Trude Blomso, David Gottlieb, Jim Hall, Ken Lee, Ann Parker, Anne and Jim Parker, David Meggyesy and Carolyn Silk, and, most enduringly and endearingly, my wife Sharon and daughter Elizabeth.

Last but just as easily first, my thanks to Mike Spinnler, the long-time JFK race director and former JFK champion whose tremendous enthusiasm has kept the torch of President Kennedy's hopes for a more physically, mentally, and morally fit country—and the legacy of America's most iconic ultramarathon—burning so brightly all these years.

ABOUT THE AUTHOR

ED AYRES has been running competitively for fifty-five con-
secutive years, and he enjoys it as much now as he did when
he joined his high school cross-country team in 1956. Ayres
placed third in the first New York Marathon in 1970, and he
is the only runner of that race still competing today. Having
participated in the early growth of American interest in road-
running, trail-running, and marathons, he also became one
of the pioneers of ultrarunning. He placed third in the US 50
Mile championship in 1976 (in 5:46:52); first in the JFK 50
Mile in 1977; and first in four US national age-division championships at 50K road, 50K trail, and fifty miles. He was the
founding editor and publisher of *Running Times* magazine,
and he also worked for thirteen years as the editorial director
of the Worldwatch Institute.